PRAYING WITH
POWER

women of faith™

PRAYING WITH POWER

BY

CHRISTA KINDE

FOREWORD BY

PATSY CLAIRMONT

THOMAS NELSON
Since 1798

CONTENTS

⚐ Foreword ⚐

I confess it is my tendency to scamper about in my world like the time-driven rabbit from Alice in Wonderland. A lot of folks think I sport ten-speed tennis shoes because I'm constantly shifting into high gear leaving behind my signature in a trail of skid marks. So you can only imagine how difficult it is when you add my proclivity for lights, camera, to my action-packed life, to park long enough to pray. And while I have found it goes against my wiring to pause and ponder I've also found it's hazardous not to. I mean left to my own devices, I'm dangerous. Besides I'd wear out all my parts in no time the way I beat a path. Prayer is my link to sanity, stability, and longevity.

Am I suggesting we live longer when we pray? Possibly. There's nothing like quiet reflective moments to encourage our blood pressures to stop percolating, our hearts to fall back into rhythm, and our minds to stop gyrating. Then add to all of that the untold benefits of loving exchanges with our all-knowing, all-seeing, all-powerful God. He who assigns our days and redeems our losses has a way of calming our anxieties and even healing our infirmities.

I love that the Lord is not only hospitable but He is invitational. That's probably why he is said to be "The Door." Jesus makes our entrance to the Father possible. He knew we would need time in His presence where we could step out of the whirlwind and into His consoling company. It is there, as we lean our heads upon his breast, that we are both deeply heard and deeply understood.

In the pages ahead we will explore journaling prayers, prayer attitudes, and how to pray our way through a desert or a valley. We'll also get up-close and personal in Two-way Conversations and learn how to survive and yes, even enjoy, those times when we're put on the spot to pray out loud. Eek! We'll learn how God answers us even when we can't hear Him saying a thing and we'll be reminded that we never grow so old that we don't need to take time to say "thank you."

Listen, why don't we park our Reeboks®, turn off our cellphones (Please!), and allow the tension in our encumbered shoulders to begin to melt away. There is One who awaits us, delights in us, and longs for our undivided attention. And I don't know about you but in this tainted world (and I'm one of the tainters), I need some holy moments. I need my sin-sick heart washed cleaner than the fresh fallen snow outside my winter window. I long for the heavenly perspective that allows me to see beyond my stuck places. I even welcome divine correction where I've stepped off the path so I can find my way back. And I desire to recognize more quickly the eternal voice of the Lord over the din of this world and the racket in my head.

So please friends, come join me as we learn how to enter the privileged sanctuary of prayer.

—*Patsy Clairmont*

INTRODUCTION

*Prayer is reaching out to touch Someone—namely, your
Creator. In the process He touches you.*

—Barbara Johnson

What's the big deal about prayer? We know we should all do it more often, take it more seriously, and give it more time—but we don't. Does this mean prayer is optional? After all, some of the other spiritual disciplines seem pretty outdated, like fasting and solitude. Who has time for that? That kind of stuff is for monks, nuns, and pastors. We've gotten along okay without it.

So, does prayer fit into the non-essentials of the Christian walk? Prayer must be an "in case of emergency" last resort kind of spiritual tool. Right?

No way!

Prayer isn't some kind of requirement for believers. It is a privilege! You have the ear of the Divine. Prayer is our path to the adventure of building a relationship with our Savior.

God knows what's going on in your life. The Creator of everything stoops to hear the lisping of toddlers. The Sustainer of every living thing hears the groans and sighs of the aging. He is aware of every thought, every choice, every move you make—but He is waiting for you to turn to Him and tell Him about it.

God listens to you. He will answer you.

Come and listen, all you who fear God, and I will tell you what he did for me. For I cried out to him for help, praising him as I spoke. If I had not confessed the sin in my heart, my Lord would not have listened. But God did listen! He paid attention to my prayer. Praise God, who did not ignore my prayer and did not withdraw his unfailing love from me.

Psalm 66:16–20, NLT

CHAPTER ONE

CALL TO ME

"CALL TO ME, AND I WILL ANSWER YOU, AND SHOW YOU GREAT AND MIGHTY THINGS, WHICH YOU DO NOT KNOW."

Jeremiah 33:3, NKJV

*J*ohn says the only reason we love God is because He first loved us. In the same way, we could not pray to our Heavenly Father if He had not first asked us to do so. "Call to me," invites our Heavenly Father. It is an invitation to pray. He has made Himself available to us 24/7/365. He has put out the welcome mat. He has given us the green light. We have a direct line to His throne room. We have a permission slip, a backstage pass, an engraved invitation. He has an open door policy for all of His children. And when we do call out His name, He gives us His undivided attention.

1. Prayer doesn't just happen. We must take a little initiative. But we can pray because God has invited our prayers. What does Psalm 50:15 declare?

CLEARING THE COBWEBS

Who is the first person you turn to when you have a piece of wonderful news to share? Your mother? Your sister? Your best friend?

> *The joy and pleasure of speaking with the Lord is far superior to anything life on this earth affords. Through prayer I become centered and serene. When it's quiet and still, I sense the Lord comes near as I enter His presence.*
>
> Luci Swindoll

2. Believe it or not, the Bible does share just one definite rule regarding prayer. You can find it in Exodus 23:13. What is God's command in this verse?

3. David understood the importance of this. What are his words of promise to God in Psalm 5:2?

> *Wouldn't it be horrible if Jesus slept through some events in our lives? We would call Him, but He couldn't hear the call because He was trying to rest. Wouldn't it be frightening to think He could forget our requests? Wouldn't it be tragic if He were so busy He couldn't remember what we talked to Him about? Thank God we don't have to endure that kind of treatment from our Lord!*
>
> Thelma Wells

4. In the beginning, prayer wasn't needed, for Adam walked through the garden paths with God, in the cool of the evening. This gave him a chance to talk things over with his Maker face to face. But when sin entered the world, and the population began to explode, things changed. What does Genesis 4:26 say began to happen about the time Adam's grandkids were being born?

5. In Psalm 116:10, David says, "I believed in you, so I prayed" (NLT). Belief—faith—is at the foundation of prayer. Christians believe God has invited them to call upon Him. They trust Him to listen to their prayers and to answer. What does this say about the believer who does not pray?

What's the purpose of prayer? Why is it so important? Why do we do it? There are plenty of reasons. Prayer reacquaints us with our Savior, solidifies our relationship with Him. Prayer reaffirms His Lordship in our lives, welcomes His input, familiarizes us with His voice, calms our frazzled emotions, lifts our eyes beyond our daily struggles. Prayer underscores God's omnipotence, highlights His patient care, acknowledges God's wisdom, recognizes His sovereignty, appeals to His mercy, magnifies His name. Why do you pray?

6. What reason did David give for praying in Psalm 17:6?

Prayer is the place where burdens are shifted. Have you ever experienced the joy of coming alongside Jesus, lining up your shoulder next to His? He puts an arm around you, pulling you close. He speaks words of life into your ears, supporting your back under the stuff you are carrying. By the end of the trail you realize the stuff has shifted. It doesn't seem so heavy anymore. Surprised, you look up to see that Jesus has gone on ahead of you, with the heaviest part of your burden squarely atop His shoulders.

Barbara Johnson

7. God's love inspires our devotion and calls our hearts into prayer. How does Psalm 42:8 describe the give and take of David's prayer life? What has God done? How does David respond?

> When Scripture states He watches over us and will not slumber, I'm thrilled to realize that should I wake up in the night, He's awake too. Some of my best times with Him have occurred during the wee hours of the morning when no one else is alert. I've settled enormous issues during some of those nocturnal chats. Other times I've just felt comforted by His presence. Sometimes there's no talk at all. I just know He's there.
>
> Marilyn Meberg

8. God's ears are always tuned to our hearts. He is faithful to hear and answer our prayers. What is the psalmist's resolution in Psalm 116:2?

DIGGING DEEPER

Every Psalm is a prayer of sorts, whether David is pleading with God or singing His praises. Many of these Psalms give us a glimpse of God's invitation to prayer. Others are requests by David for God to hear him out and to answer his call. Let's look at a few of these verses in the Psalms, to remind ourselves God is near.

- Psalm 65:2   • Psalm 86:7   • Psalm 91:15   • Psalm 143:1

PONDER & PRAY

Paul was a communicator. He kept in touch with fellow believers, many of whom he had fathered in faith. He wrote letters, filled with words of wisdom, advice, correction, and praise. He spoke God's truth, answered troublesome questions, greeted dear friends, and encouraged Christians everywhere. But if you take a careful look through Paul's epistles, you will also find his prayers. Each week as we delve into our own prayer lives, we will sneak a peek at Paul's. In this "Ponder and Pray" section, one of Paul's prayers will be printed, and you are invited to pray his prayer after him by rewriting it in your own words. Change it. Personalize it. Make it your own.

We pray that you will be strengthened with His glorious power so that you will have all the patience and endurance you need. May you be filled with joy. —Colossians 1:11, NLT

By way of example, here is my prayer. Add your own below.

*D*ear Father, I am asking You for a boost. Your power is so vast and glorious, and I need some of it today. The only way I can face my day's work cheerfully, enduring the routine, is by Your power. The only way I can find the patience to show kindness to my family today is if You lend me Your own strength. And in whatever I may face today, help me to see the humor, give me a glimpse of glory, and settle my soul in contentment—for then I shall surely have joy. Amen.

TRINKETS TO TREASURE

At the close of each lesson, you will be presented with a small gift. Though imaginary, it will serve to remind you of the things you have learned. Think of it as a souvenir! Souvenirs are little trinkets we pick up on our journeys to remind us of where we have been. They keep us from forgetting the path we have traveled. Hide these little treasures in your heart, for as you ponder on them, they will draw you closer to God!

Your trinket for this week is a reminder that God wants you to call upon Him. It's an invitation. He has invited you to come to Him in prayer. God has made Himself available to you, and awaits your call. Your invitation is the key to His undivided attention. So set your mind on Him, let Him know how much you love Him, and pour out your heart. He wants to hear it all.

NOTES & PRAYER REQUESTS

CHAPTER TWO

BOLDLY GO

"LET US THEREFORE COME BOLDLY TO THE THRONE
OF GRACE, THAT WE MAY OBTAIN MERCY AND FIND
GRACE TO HELP IN TIME OF NEED."

Hebrews 4:16, NKJV

Nothing is more disagreeable than a bold child—the kind who will march right up to you and call you by your first name. It's just too shocking for words. Of course, I was raised in Minnesota, and in the northern reaches, it's considered most respectful to refer to adults as "Mr. Johnson" or "Mrs. Peterson." I was only on a first-name basis with my little sister. And so, my children were likewise trained. It didn't matter if their Sunday school teacher's last name was a mouthful. With a little coaching, they can manage "Mrs. Kamyszek."

Then, we moved south, and suddenly the world of politeness took a turn. In this warm and hospitable place, respect has taken on the soft drawls of "Mister Lee" and "Miss Teri." Even when I tried to stick to the way I was raised, folks would quietly correct me. Nobody wants to be Mr.'d or Mrs.'d in Tennessee. So I am resigned to

CLEARING THE COBWEBS

How can you show both boldness and respect at the same time?

7

my children, with a mixture of boldness and respect, calling our friends by their first names—with the appropriate "Miss" and "Mister" tagged on.

To think, they could have called Mrs. Kamyszek "Miss Cathy" down here. It would have been so much easier!

One of the most touching scriptures is Galatians 4:6, in which God says to us, "Because you are sons, God sent the Spirit of his Son into our hearts, the Spirit who calls out 'Abba, Father.'" The Hebrew word abba means "daddy." We are reminded that we are never totally fatherless, and in times of quiet despair, we can cry out a prayer like this: "Daddy, oh, Daddy, comfort me, hold me. I so need Your touch. I so need Your tender presence. Be with me, dear Daddy. Let me rest in You, relax in You, and find peace in You."

Marilyn Meberg

1. The Jews were so fearful of offending God and showing Him the utmost respect, they would not even say His name. On the other hand, Jesus, showing sinless respect at all times, called God Abba, or "Daddy." How do you tend to think of God? Is there a measure of fear blended with familiarity?

2. Though we are welcomed to call Him our Father and our Friend, God is still to be feared. What does Psalm 33:8 say about God?

3. Let's look at another description of our loving Heavenly Father. What does James, the brother of Jesus, point out about God in James 2:19?

4. Solomon, in all his great wisdom, boiled down the purpose of the human race in Ecclesiastes: "Fear God and keep His commandments. For this is man's all" (Eccl. 12:13, NKJV). God specifically required fear from His people. What did He ask of them in Deuteronomy 10:12–13?

5. Boldness is not the same as arrogance. God waits for the prayers of a humble heart. How does Ezra refer to himself when he speaks to God? His prayer is found in Ezra 9:6.

6. Isaiah pleads for mercy: "Oh, don't be so angry with us, Lord. Please don't remember our sins forever" (Is. 64:9, NLT). According to Acts 8:22, what must a Christian do in order to restore a right relationship with the Lord?

Have you ever attempted to get in touch with God and found yourself doubting His ability to help you? Do you find yourself worrying about things you should tell God about instead? Do you feel ashamed to talk to God? Do you find yourself seeking other people's opinions rather than relying on God's guidance? Do you think you have to use a certain posture or language to get God's attention? Do you think you've done something so awful you can't tell God? If your answer is yes to any of those questions, you're creating unnecessary interference between you and God. Nothing can keep you from being directly connected to God if you want to be.

Thelma Wells

7. First Kings 8:30 and 2 Chronicles 7:14 are two very good examples of the fact God has been showing mercy to sinners for centuries now. What does God ask of the confessor? What does God promise to do if these conditions are met?

Remember when Crayola™ markers started coming out in special color combinations? You could still buy the classic colors of the rainbow, but there was also the option of purchasing a package of all pastel colors, or a package designated "bold." Are you a pastel package kind of gal? Or do you like to let loose with the bold set of markers? I've known both kinds of people.

One sweet lady I know looks like a watercolor painting—soft blue eyes, porcelain skin, blonde hair that's almost white. Everything she loves would have to have the word "light," "pale," "soft," or "icy" put in front of its color. She drives a powder blue car. Her bedroom walls could be described as "whisper of lilac." Her world is quiet, and she collects Precious Moments figurines.

Then, there's this guy I went to college with. He wore such vividly colored shirts that they easily earned the adjective loud. Before they were ever stylish, he was wearing colors which made people squint. One shirt had comic strips on it, another had sunglasses scattered over it. I think I remember a shirt with planets and stars on it. He had the most outrageous taste. But his style suited his outgoing personality and quirky sense of humor. He played the saxophone, and gathered a wide circle of friends.

> I have a basket at my tubside filled with cleaning utensils: sponges, brushes, loofahs, pumice, and soaps. As helpful as these items are, they do not compare to how clean I feel when I have spent moments in the Lord's presence, especially when I begin with a confession time.
>
> Patsy Clairmont

Whatever your color preference might be, Jesus has invited you to come into the hush of His Father's throne room with all the boldness of a loud shirt. He won't be startled. You are there at His Son's invitation. And whether you're wearing icy pink or tangerine, He sees you robed in righteousness.

8. Having been forgiven, we are welcomed into the very courts of heaven. What does the writer of Hebrews 4:16 say we will obtain there?

I can still picture my mom using a washboard to deal with tough stains on my dad's work clothes. Our Heavenly Father doesn't have to haul out a washboard when He sees our stubbornly stained hearts. We enter the inner room when we plead the blood of Jesus, and our filthy sins become as white as snow in His presence (and that, my friends, is better than a Good Housekeeping seal of approval).

Patsy Clairmont

9. We may tremble in the face of God's greatness, but we can also have confidence in our welcome. David had confidence in God's faithfulness in keeping His word. And his trust affected his prayers: "O Lord Almighty, God of Israel, I have been bold enough to pray this prayer because You have revealed that you will build a house for me—an eternal dynasty!" (2 Sam. 7:27, NLT). Do you have boldness when you pray? What kinds of assurances has God made to you? Let's take a look:

Psalm 32:1 _____

Psalm 103:12 _____

John 15:15_____

Romans 8:15 _____

Romans 8:26 _____

Hebrews 7:25 _____

God is always on duty in the temple of your heart, His home. You needn't be stiff and formal when you pray. Simply make yourself cozy in the old rocking chair of trust, pulling the afghan of faith around you, and then talk to God.

Barbara Johnson

DIGGING DEEPER

In the presence of God's holiness, men fell to the ground, hid their faces, and cried out in fear. Why? Here are some verses which shed light on their holy terror. As you consider these verses, realize that the very God who makes the earth tremble with dread is the God who loves you completely, provided for your salvation, and calls you His own.

- Psalm 99:1
- Jeremiah 10:10
- Hebrews 12:28
- Psalm 114:7 • Isaiah 8:13
- Daniel 6:26 • Hebrews 10:31

PONDER & PRAY

Pray this prayer after Paul. Rewrite it in your own words, applying it to your own heart.

I pray that your hearts will be flooded with light so that you can understand the wonderful future He has promised to those He called. I want you to realize what a rich and glorious inheritance He has given to His people.—Ephesians 1:18, NLT

TRINKETS TO TREASURE

Whenever I think of boldness, I think of the old saying "bold as brass." So your trinket for the week is a little brass button. God deserves your respect, to be sure. But the Father has assured you your welcome is secure. There is no fear for God's own child to come before His throne. So, trust God to be true to His word, and find yourself ushered into the very throne room of heaven when you pray.

NOTES & PRAYER REQUESTS

CHAPTER THREE

TEACH US TO PRAY

"NOW IT CAME TO PASS, AS HE WAS PRAYING IN A
CERTAIN PLACE, WHEN HE CEASED, THAT ONE OF
HIS DISCIPLES SAID TO HIM, 'LORD, TEACH US TO
PRAY.'"

Luke 11:1, NKJV

*I*n many ways, I take after my father—both in looks and mindset. But I am my mother's daughter in the kitchen. We are by no means gourmet chefs, but when it comes to putting on a good old-fashioned meat-and-potatoes kind of meal, we're pros. My Mom can put on a meal for twenty-odd people without blinking an eye, and I have the dubious distinction of being called "Queen of Gravy." But, neither of us uses recipes. We're of the old school—a little of this and a little of that until it feels just right and then it's done.

I married into a family of equally good cooks. Wonderful meals, and good home cooking—but recipe-users the whole lot of them. These folks had carefully perfected all their secret recipes (one-half cup, plus two teaspoons sugar). They would experiment by making recipes two different ways, or in two different pans, then taste-test them to see which was better. Nothing was left to chance. The eggs must be medium—not large. The milk must

CLEARING ↗ THE ↖ COBWEBS

Do you have a favorite dish you cook so often that you don't even have to look at the recipe anymore? What is it?

be whole milk, at room temperature. The whipping process must go on for twenty-five minutes, not one minute less or the consistency would be off.

With the Lord's Prayer in Matthew 6 and Luke 11, Jesus gives us a recipe for prayer. Most of us have it memorized. But He didn't mean for us to stick to the recipe as given every time we pray. Even I use the recipe the first time I make a dish. Then, once I've got the gist of it, I just throw it together the next time. Jesus' prayer is a guideline, a lesson about prayer. But God welcomes our own creative touches when we come to Him to share our hearts.

> *We are admonished to pray without ceasing because prayers assert God's power in our lives. When we fail to pray, we aren't cheating God; we're cheating ourselves.*
>
> Thelma Wells

1. How long have you known the Lord's Prayer? Who taught you?

2. We have God's attention, and we are invited to pray. So what do we say to God? The Lord's Prayer is Jesus' example of how we should pray. Did you know He also gives us some negative examples, of how we should not pray? Look at one in Luke 18:11–14. What is the difference between the prayer of the Pharisee and the prayer of the tax collector?

3. Look up Matthew 6:7. What is the other definite don't that Jesus shares with His disciples.

4. There are so many things we can pray about; they cannot be numbered. Here are a few of the things the Bible mentions through its pages—the prayers of others often inspire and encourage our own prayer life. Match the text in the first column with the matter of prayer in the second column which is mentioned in its passage.

___ 1 Samuel 1:27	a. strength for the work before you
___ 2 Kings 6:17	b. those in authority over us
___ Ezra 8:21	c. protection from evil people
___ Nehemiah 6:9	d. safety in travel
___ Jeremiah 42:2–3	e. a chance to see dear friends again
___ Matthew 19:13	f. direction
___ Romans 1:10	g. to have a baby
___ Romans 12:14	h. blessings for our children
___ 2 Thessalonians 3:2	i. good health
___ 1 Timothy 2:2	j. wisdom
___ James 1:5	k. ability to see things as they are
___ 3 John 1:2	l. blessings for our persecutors

5. The Scriptures encourage us to pray for one another—for our brothers and sisters in Christ. Paul's heart was especially dedicated to prayer for his fellow Christians. What does he write in Romans 1:9?

6. On a larger scale, we need to be praying for the work of the Lord to continue.

> My friend Ney said something that made me suddenly very quiet at the center of my soul: "I learned years ago not to edit my prayers." She explained that her job is to "make her requests known," as a child would, and then, no matter the result, trust that God is praised and honored.
>
> Marilyn Meberg

*D*o you pray for your pastor? What does Colossians 4:4 encourage us to pray on his behalf?

Do you pray for those who do not know the Lord? What does 1 Timothy 2:1 urge us to do on their behalf?

Do you pray for missionaries and evangelists? What does Colossians 4:3 ask us to include in our prayers?

7. What does Philippians 4:6 tell us we should pray about?

> *Pray confidently. But be careful what you pray for—because everything and anything is possible through the power of prayer.*
>
> Barbara Johnson

8. There are times when we can't quite put our feelings into words. There are times when we feel a prompting to pray, but we do not know what to say. There are times when our burdens and grief are so great, we cannot even form our thoughts. According to Romans 8:26, what provision has God made for us in these times?

*W*e have a son who is, apparently, defective. We didn't realize it until he was two, and beginning to talk. You see, he came without a volume control. With this boy, it is either loud, or asleep (and even then he snores!). Being a little further down the line in the family birth order, he learned very early, he had to speak up to be heard. Since his vocabulary is limited, his main tactic is to repeat a short phrase over and over until he drowns out all other conversation. At this point, he gets what he needs. So whether we're at the table or in the car, he'll begin. "I'm thirsty. I'm thirsty. I'm thirsty." (It actually comes out "shirshty"). Or "My blanket. My blanket. My blanket." until someone hands him his favorite blanket. If nothing else, he's persistent. I wonder if this is how we sound to our Heavenly Father when we are in need. "Help me. Help me. Help me."

Jesus could be persistent in His prayer, too. Matthew 26:44 says He brought His needs to His Father three times, saying the same things over each time. God didn't mind that. God answered His Son by giving Him the peace and strength He needed for the day ahead of Him. God will answer your calling, too.

9. Jesus gives us a parable on prayer in Luke 11:5–13. What quality in prayer gets results?

10. Do you dread asking for patience because you'd rather avoid situations where your patience will be tested? Do you hold back asking God to show you His will for your life, just in case He might ask you to do something you'd rather not? Now consider the rest of the paragraph in Luke 11. Jesus again issues a wide-open invitation. Ask! Seek! Knock! What will be the result of these persistent prayers?

Shielding our loved ones from the consequences of their problems often isn't possible. But praying for their ability to handle those problems is appropriate and can benefit them and us. If you're trying to accept responsibility for the problems of others, pray for them and pray with them—without ceasing.

Thelma Wells

DIGGING DEEPER

Paul encourages Christians to make persistent prayer a way of life. Five different times he tells us to make our prayer life a ceaseless one. Take a look at these verses. What kinds of things is Paul praying about in these various texts?

- Romans 1:9
- 1 Thessalonians 2:13
- 1 Timothy 1:3
- 1 Thessalonians 1:3
- 1 Thessalonians 5:17

PONDER & PRAY

Paul's prayers captured so much of the essence of living the Christian life. Take this verse from Philippians and transform it into your own prayer.

I pray that your love for each other will overflow more and more, and that you will keep on growing in your knowledge and understanding.—Philippians 1:9, NLT

TRINKETS TO TREASURE

Jesus gave us the Lord's Prayer as an example of how to pray—a recipe if you will. So our trinket this week is a recipe card. Go ahead and print the Lord's Prayer onto your card. Keeping His method in mind, you can play with the recipe, making it your own whenever you pray. Pray about the cares you have on hand, avoiding showiness and babbling. Instead, use a good measure of humility and a dash of persistence.

Notes & Prayer Requests

CHAPTER FOUR

PRAYER CLOSETS

"HE WENT IN ALONE AND SHUT THE DOOR BEHIND HIM AND PRAYED TO THE LORD."

2 Kings 4:33, NLT

When it comes to prayer, mothers of preschoolers have their work cut out for them. In the first place, they are never alone. They barely have time to bathe some days, let alone find a quiet hour for prayer. Days are full and sleep is precious. A mom has to be creative to carve out some prayer time. Some moms find a harbor of rest during naptime. (I always seemed to need a nap, too.) When my girls were little, they would tag-team their naps. When one got up, the other went down. It was impossible to get alone. What I wouldn't have given to sublet Superman's Fortress of Solitude. Some days, I wished I even had the closet space to shut myself in for a few hours, I was so desperate for peace.

What worked for me came in the form of a video ballet lesson and two pink tutus. Every morning after breakfast, two little ballerinas would line up for their arabesques, happily twirling around the family room for a full thirty minutes. It wasn't long, but it was enough.

CLEARING ⊀ THE ⊱ COBWEBS

Do you have someplace you go when you want to be alone? Where is that quiet place?

You may not have an easy time finding your prayer closet or your quiet time, but it's worth the effort. Figure out what works for you, then meet the Lord there.

1. When do you pray?

2. Everyone has their own way of doing things—their own routine. Even throughout the pages of the Bible, faithful followers of God met with Him in different ways. Look up the following verses, and jot down a few lines about the prayer habits of God's people.

Daniel in Daniel 6:10 _____

Jesus in Mark 1:35 _____

Jesus in Luke 6:12 _____

Cornelius in Acts 10:2 _____

Paul and Silas in Acts 16:25 _____

Paul in 1 Thessalonians 3:10 _____

My times of silence before God are very important to me. I put everything else down, every word away, and I am with the Lord. When I'm quiet, life falls into perspective for me. I have a very active mind and I'm a worrier, but in those moments when I choose to put that away, I rest beside the Shepherd in still places.

Sheila Walsh

3. Read 1 Kings 8:59. What did Solomon hope would become of his prayer?

4. How does Paul encourage us to pray? Check in Ephesians 6:18 for his familiar admonition.

5. Paul encourages the people in one of his churches, "We always pray for you" (Col. 1:3, NLT). Do you have people who are always in your prayers? Who?

> *In quiet conversations with our Lord, we hear in our longing hearts of His expansive love, which helps us to move from our inner conflict to His peaceful resolution.*
>
> Patsy Clairmont

*I*n our hectic days and busy lives, we long to come away into a quiet place with God. Oh, to escape for a season, live like a monk, and get things straightened out with the Lord! But in the hustle and bustle of our weeks, we cannot find time for a divine rendezvous. Sadly, most of us simply shrug our shoulders and keep moving. Since there's no time slot available, we are off the hook! God probably understands.

But God doesn't like that option. Neither will you once you are burned out, weary, and longing for His peace. Those times of communion with God give us strength for our days, nourish our souls, and keep our perspectives in tune with God's. Without His touch, we lose focus, feel overwhelmed, and stumble through our days.

So if you can't manage a rendezvous with God, might I suggest a few stolen moments!

Prayer doesn't have to be longwinded to be effective. You don't need long weekends and quiet cathedrals to connect with God. Look for some nooks and crannies—in line at the grocery store, while you wash your hands, waiting at a red light, while you tie your shoes, whenever you climb the stairs, while you make photocopies, as you sweep the floor. Infuse your day with prayer.

6. Getting alone with God is basic to nurturing your prayer life. Others have learned the lesson of solitude. One way or another, they drew apart in order to pray. Look up these verses and make a note of where these believers went in order to get some privacy.

Jonah 2:1 _____

Matthew 14:23 _____

Mark 6:46 _____

Luke 5:16 _____

Luke 18:10 _____

Luke 22:41 _____

Acts 10:9 _____

Revelation 1:9–10 _____

7. Do you have a regular rendezvous point with God? Where do you go to pray?

It doesn't matter what time of day or night it is, what day of the week it is, who else is talking to Him, or what the problem is. He is always available to listen and to help us without static or interference. His omnipotence has blocked out anything and everything that would keep Him from hearing and answering us.

Thelma Wells

8. Are you ever tempted to announce to the room that you'll be just over there for the next hour, praying, should you be needed? Jesus warns us not to make a show of our prayers. Read Matthew 6:5–6. How do the hypocrites behave?

9. What is the reward these show-offs gain?

10. In contrast, what does Jesus encourage us to do when we pray?

If we would just wait on God, let the silence fall, we could be gifted with the response of a loving Father to His children. In that holy moment we could receive a beatitude, a blessing that no human words could begin to frame.

Sheila Walsh

DIGGING DEEPER

One of the reasons we need a quiet place to pray is because God's answers are often quiet. We must be still in order to follow His lead. All the distractions of life pull us away from His prompting. When you feel the pull of the Lord on your heart, heed His call and withdraw into your prayer closet.

Let's explore a few verses today which show us God's quiet ways:

- 1 Kings 19:12
- Isaiah 30:15
- 1 Thessalonians 4:11
- 1 Timothy 2:2
- 1 Peter 3:4

PONDER & PRAY

Paul has such a way with words. Consider the imagery in this prayer of his, then make it your own by rewriting it.

And I pray that Christ will be more and more at home in your hearts as you trust in Him. May your roots go down deep into the soil of God's marvelous love. —Ephesians 3:17, NLT

TRINKETS TO TREASURE

As you search out a quiet place this week, take along this trinket—a set of earplugs. Even in the noisiest of households or the busiest public place, we can find a tiny pool of peace when we turn our thoughts towards God. Seek out and designate your prayer closet this week (if you don't already have one) and then make the decision to get into it on a daily basis. These times of solitude and prayer will become precious to you and to your Heavenly Father.

Notes & Prayer Requests

CHAPTER FIVE

TWO-WAY CONVERSATIONS

"O EARTH, EARTH, EARTH, HEAR THE WORD OF THE LORD!"

Jeremiah 22:29, NKJV

*L*istening in on a one-sided phone conversation can be so frustrating. Though we try to pick up cues and clues from the speaker we can see, our understanding is severely limited. Over the years, I have gotten good at putting together the pieces of my husband's half-heard phone conversations. When he's speaking to a woman, his tone of voice gets higher and gentler. When it's a man on the other end of the line, there's a more macho bass rumble to his replies. Certain references indicate a work-related call, others are a telltale sign it's a family member. A prolonged silence paired with a bored expression is a sure sign that he's hooked up with a salesperson. They talk so fast, without taking a breath, it's hard to inform them you are uninterested in their product and still remain polite.

Too often our prayer lives become one-sided. We do all the talking, but never pause to let God get a word in edgewise. We trundle on in a blithe monologue, but never pause to hear what God

CLEARING THE COBWEBS

What is your favorite avenue of communication—one-on-one conversation, group chit-chat, telephone calls, letters, email? How do you like to keep in touch with those closest to you?

might have to say to us. Prayer isn't supposed to be talking *to* God, but talking with God. As a conversation, a dialogue, it becomes necessary to stop speaking, and listen.

1. There is a danger in doing all the talking when you pray. You aren't allowing your Father to have any input in the conversation. Have you ever stopped to wonder—if you are not pausing to listen to God, then who *are* you listening to? John cautions Christians to pay attention to whom they listen. What are our two choices according to 1 John 4:5–6?

> *God is offering Himself to you at a generous exchange rate: His forgiveness for your sins, His joy for your grief, His love for your loneliness. You will grow rich as you spend time with Him, listening for His voice.*
>
> Barbara Johnson

2. So how does God "talk back" to us in our times of prayer? Romans 8:14 hints at one way.

3. What is the primary way in which we hear the voice of God? Romans 10:17 tells us clearly.

4. Proverbs 30:5 states "Every word of God is pure." But can words written down centuries ago be relevant now? How can they be considered part of a conversation we're having now?

*P*rayer goes hand in hand with our daily Bible reading. God wants us to study His Word, approaching our Bibles attentively—actively listening, seeking God's words for us. Here we find the topic of our day's conversations with Him.

This is called our "quiet time" for a good reason. "Quiet," because the noisy world we live in drowns out the Spirit's promptings and the Savior's call. We must learn to slow down, to settle ourselves so we can hear. And "time" because study, prayer, and worship all take time. Too often we exchange our daily bread for a daily crouton when it comes to Bible reading. Don't rush through a chapter and verse so you can check it off your list and move on to the next thing. Don't hurry past the words you know to be "living and powerful" and able to change you. Spend *time* with the Word. Steep in it. Soak in it. Tell Him what you see. Ask Him how it pertains to your situation. Listen for God's leading.

When I first began to give myself to the discipline of solitude I despaired of ever being able to quiet my mind. I would turn the radio or TV off and sit for a while. My mind would wander all over the place. I found myself thinking about what I would make for dinner. I was repeatedly discouraged, wanting to quit, reasoning that this was simply not the way for me to fellowship with God. But I didn't give up. I kept trying. After a while I began to relax into being alone with God. I left all my lists and requests behind. This was time for quiet, not for petition.

Sheila Walsh

5. How does 1 Thessalonians 2:13 describe the Word of God?

You can stop and listen to God every day, quiet your spirit before Him, ask Him to communicate with you. God has plenty to say to you, but He requires your undivided attention. Psalm 46:10 tells us that we will know God and His sovereignty when we are "still." Be still and know His will for you today.

Thelma Wells

6. Several of the writers of the Scriptures we now carry mentioned why they committed the words of God to paper. What were their reasonings according to these verses?

David in Psalm 102:18 _____

John in John 20:31 _____

Paul in Romans 15:4 _____

John again in 1 John 5:13 _____

7. When Joshua takes the leadership of God's people after Moses' death, God makes His expectations clear. According to Joshua 1:8, what does God expect Joshua to do with his "Bible"?

When you need to make decisions and nobody on earth understands, call Him up. When your problems seem unbearable, call Him up. When you want to praise Him and show appreciation for His wonderful work in your life, call Him up. When you want to communicate with someone who wants to communicate with you and who has all the answers to your questions, call Him up.

Thelma Wells

8. First Peter 1:23 says we have been born again, "through the word of God which lives and abides forever" (NKJV). According to Revelation 19:13, how can we be very certain the Word of God is eternal?

Digging Deeper

The Bible is filled with warning for those who do not listen, or do not want to hear God's words. Ignoring the truth will never make it go away. God's Word will stand in the end. These verses provide a sobering reminder that we must hold close to the Word of the Lord—listening and obeying:

- Jeremiah 6:10
- John 14:24
- Ezekiel 13:2
- 1 Peter 2:8
- John 14:15

Ponder & Pray

Sometimes I think Paul must have had some inkling of the internal struggles we face every day. His prayers, though often short, encourage us in the midst of our complicated lives. Here is one to rewrite into your own prayer.

So we keep on praying for you, that our God will make you worthy of the life to which He called you. And we pray that God, by His power, will fulfill all your good intentions and faithful deeds. —2 Thessalonians 1:11, NLT

Trinkets to Treasure

Learning to be a good listener is one of the hardest lessons of being a good communicator. There are times when we need to bite our tongue, hold our peace, zip our lip, and put a cork in it. With this in mind, our trinket for the week is a cork. Consider it a gentle reminder not to talk God's ear off without giving Him the courtesy of a chance to speak as well. In your quiet times, listen for His leading and soak yourself in the Scriptures. That's where your chance to talk to God becomes an opportunity to talk *with* God.

NOTES & PRAYER REQUESTS

CHAPTER SIX

JOURNALING
PRAYERS

"OH, THAT MY WORDS WERE WRITTEN!
OH, THAT THEY WERE INSCRIBED IN A BOOK!"

Job 19:23, NKJV

*T*here is so much in life to keep track of. Names, dates, addresses, and phone numbers. Appointments, agendas, allergies, anniversaries. Shoe sizes, due dates, business receipts, and grocery lists. Ink cartridges, calorie counters, nursery schedules, secret family recipes. Phone messages, passwords, pin numbers, and prescriptions.

And so we make careful lists. We have appointment books, address books, telephone books, and recipe books. We write down grocery lists and to do lists. We trade business cards. We plot our lives on a calendar. We keep a record of everything that is important and essential to living.

But do you keep a spiritual journal? A record of your walk with the Lord—lessons learned, Scriptures memorized, uplifted prayers, and joys along life's journey. Many women take the time each day to write a letter to God. With pen in hand they pour out their hearts to their Father,

CLEARING
⟋ THE ⟍
COBWEBS

Based on your interests and the experiences of your life, what sort of book would you write, if you could?

and at the same time keep a lasting record of their relationship with Him.

> There are many benefits to journaling, but for me one stands out above all the rest. I put a premium upon knowing one's self, and the blank pages of a journal give me a place to become better acquainted with me. I can explore my own feelings and questions, or come to grips with my own confusion or angst. I can cry as I write, or laugh. I can sort through my life's experiences and gain understanding about myself. I can privately wrestle with personal issues and conflicts.
>
> Luci Swindoll

1. What would you write down in a spiritual journal? Why would you keep one?

2. Whether we are mulling it over, thinking it through, rolling it around in our mind, contemplating, pondering, puzzling, musing, or brooding, God wants us to be meditating on His Word. Writing down our insights about the Scriptures allows us to pursue a line of thought. It's like meditation on paper. Look up the following passages from the Psalms. What do they tell us about when and what our thoughts should linger on?

Psalm 63:6 _____

Psalm 77:12 _____

Psalm 119:48 _____

Psalm 119:148 _____

Psalm 143:5 _____

3. Keeping our mind occupied with God's Word and His working in our lives serves to protect us from pondering over inappropriate things. What direction does Paul send us for the meditation of our souls in Philippians 4:8?

4. According to 1 Timothy 4:15, what will be the result of our meditation?

5. In the verses surrounding 1 Timothy 4:15, what are the "things" Paul is telling Timothy to give himself to entirely? Verses 12–16 give many examples of the kinds of things our own spiritual lives should encompass as well.

6. A spiritual journal provides us with a record of our Father's love for us. Read Psalm 42:6. When does David say he most needs this chance to remember?

> Today many of us keep tabs on our prayer lives through journals in which we write our concerns, feelings, and activities, culminating in a prayer that might be two lines or two pages long. Some of us diligently keep both a life journal, in which we record life's events and our feelings, and a prayer journal, which consists of our requests and praises offered up to our Father.
>
> Patsy Clairmont

 have vivid memories of my father's Bible. I guess they are so distinct because my dad's Bible was so distinctive. It was a thick, black, hardcover Bible, held together by duct tape. He kept it on the top of the refrigerator in the kitchen. *Well-worn* would be a kind term for that Book. My dad read and reread that Bible, marking passages as he went. He used colored pencils, markers, and highlighter pens. He worked out some elaborate color-coding system which I couldn't quite grasp as a child, but I clearly remember my fascination over large blocks of orange, red, blue, and yellow text throughout its pages. I wanted to color in my Bible, too. Even when his Bible was barely holding together, dad couldn't part with it. He knew where everything was in his own Bible. He knew on which side of the page a verse could be found, which column it was in, and what color it was. That Bible held a record of his walk with God—insights, links, promises, touchstones—the culmination of years of faithful study.

When you take notes in the margins of your Bible, and pore over its pages, highlighting the verses which speak to your soul, you are creating a journal of sorts. Your own Bible becomes a record of your growing relationship with God.

7. Do you write in your Bible?

As we meditate on God's Word, we become familiar with God's heart and His ways; as we do so, we will change. The purpose of meditation is not simply to make us feel good in a noisy world; it is not a self-absorbed agenda. Rather, as we shut our mind in with God and reflect on His words, we will know Him and be changed by Him—and that is the purpose of our lives.

Sheila Walsh

8. One of the goals of our Spiritual life should be familiarity. Familiarity with our Savior. Familiarity with the voice of our Lord. Familiarity with the Bible He has given us. Familiarity with the quiet place where we retreat for daily prayer. Do you find the comfort of familiarity when you pray?

9. A written record of our walk with the Lord, of our prayer life, can become a heritage for our children and grandchildren. David said to the Lord, "I will make Your name to be remembered in all generations; Therefore the people shall praise You forever and ever" (Ps. 45:17, NKJV). What does Deuteronomy 6:7 say about teaching the next generation about God's faithfulness?

10. A prayer journal can also be an inspiration to your continuing walk. How does Paul put it in Psalm 138:3?

> *I'm an occasional scribbler of thought and prayer, not a daily one. Oh, I pray daily; I just don't record daily. In fact, for years my personal scribbles were done on the backs of envelopes, napkins, and old receipts.*
>
> Patsy Clairmont

DIGGING DEEPER

Since writing seems to be our theme for this week, take some time to ponder over the words of Paul in 2 Corinthians 3:3: "Clearly you are an epistle of Christ, ministered by us, written not with ink but by the Spirit of the living God, not on tablets of stone but on tablets of flesh, that is, of the heart" (NKJV). What does Paul mean here?

PONDER & PRAY

Sometimes the prayers of Paul are truly inspiring, for he asks on our behalf for things we did not even know we could ask for! Rewrite this prayer from Ephesians into your own words. Make it your own.

I pray that from His glorious, unlimited resources He will give you mighty inner strength through His Holy Spirit. —Ephesians 3:16, NLT

TRINKETS TO TREASURE

After this week, nothing could be more appropriate than a journal for your treasure. Let it inspire you to begin recording your prayers. Let it stand as a record of God's faithfulness to you. Take time on its pages to meditate through the Scriptures, pondering God's Word and applying it to your daily life.

NOTES & PRAYER REQUESTS

CHAPTER SEVEN

Praying Through Passages

"I REJOICE AT YOUR WORD AS ONE WHO FINDS GREAT TREASURE."

Psalm 119:162, NKJV

o you ever go through a dry time, when even reading your Bible seems dull, let alone trying to formulate meaningful prayers to your Heavenly Father? Well, don't linger in those lulls. Don't doze your way through Deuteronomy if you need encouragement from Ephesians. Next time you find yourself yawning through your quiet time, try this. Engage your mind and your spirit by praying through whole passages of Scripture. It's a way of using your creativity, applying the Word, and claiming God's promises in a fresh way.

What could be more appropriate than a few practice passages? Read the verses slowly, considering carefully what each phrase means. Then, applying them to yourself, rewrite them as a prayer.

CLEARING ↗ THE ↖ COBWEBS

What is your favorite shade of nail polish— fire engine red, hot pink, raspberry, mauve, powder pink, coral, peach, baby blue, sea foam green, sand, taupe, ivory, or old reliable clear?

I have opinions on everything and love to give them regular airings. I process information very quickly and am ready to respond almost immediately, but I am slowly learning the benefit of taking time to meditate, to really listen, and to be changed by what I hear.

Sheila Walsh

1. *Do not fret because of evildoers, nor be envious of the workers of iniquity. For they shall soon be cut down like the grass, and wither as the green herb. Trust in the Lord, and do good; dwell in the land, and feed on His faithfulness. Delight yourself also in the Lord, and He shall give you the desires of your heart. Commit your way to the Lord, Trust also in Him, and He shall bring it to pass. He shall bring forth your righteousness as the light, and your justice as the noonday. Rest in the Lord, and wait patiently for Him; Do not fret because of him who prospers in his way, because of the man who brings wicked schemes to pass. Cease from anger, and forsake wrath; do not fret—it only causes harm.* —Psalm 37:1–8, NKJV

2. *Love each other like brothers and sisters. Give each other more honor than you want for yourselves. Do not be lazy but work hard, serving the Lord with all your heart. Be joyful because you have hope. Be patient when trouble comes, and pray at all times. Share with God's people who need help. Bring strangers in need into your homes.* —Romans 12:10–13, NCV

When I prayerfully remember my shortcomings, I'm not informing the Lord of anything He doesn't already know. But when I enumerate my failings, I take responsibility before Him, and He then releases me from dirty shame, grimy guilt, and scummy sin. I am released from all my present tensions. I am cleansed in the innermost parts of my being.

Patsy Clairmont

3. You slaves must obey your earthly masters in everything you do. Try to please them all the time, not just when they are watching you. Obey them willingly because of your reverent fear of the Lord. Work hard and cheerfully at whatever you do, as though you were working for the Lord rather than for people. Remember that the Lord will give you an inheritance as your reward, and the Master you are serving is Christ.—Colossians 3:22–24, NLT

4. Therefore, brethren, having boldness to enter the Holiest by the blood of Jesus, by a new and living way which He consecrated for us, through the veil, that is, His flesh, and having a High Priest over the house of God, let us draw near with a true heart in full assurance of faith, having our hearts sprinkled from an evil conscience and our bodies washed with pure water. Let us hold fast the confession of our hope without wavering, for He who promised is faithful. And let us consider one another in order to stir up love and good works, not forsaking the assembling of ourselves together, as is the manner of some, but exhorting one another, and so much the more as you see the Day approaching.—Hebrews 10:19–25, NKJV

> *I know my husband Barry so well because I've spent so much time with him. And I get to know God as I spend time with Him, meditating on His Word. Meditating on the Word of God is a very different principle than reading the Bible or praying. When I meditate, I take perhaps just one verse and sit with it for a while and ask God to speak to me. I might keep it in my mind for the whole day.*
>
> Sheila Walsh

5. *So prepare your minds for service and have self-control. All your hope should be for the gift of grace that will be yours when Jesus Christ is shown to you. Now that you are obedient children of God do not live as you did in the past. You did not understand, so you did the evil things you wanted. But be holy in all you do, just as God, the One who called you, is holy.* —1 Peter 1:13–15, NCV

ow, when you are reading your daily devotions, take an extra pass through the passage, and make it into your prayer. Apply God's promises to your day. Ask Him to remind you of His commands, and to help you to obey them. Confess your shortcomings, your weaknesses, and your sins—your Bible will surely bring them to light. Lean on His Word, and trust that what He has said is true.

DIGGING DEEPER

Psalm 119 is a chapter in the Bible that rains down praises on the Word of God. Many of its verses are familiar and precious. Though the entirety of Psalm 119 is worth reading—all 176 verses—here are a few selections.

- Psalm 119:11
- Psalm 119:114

- Psalm 119:50
- Psalm 119:133

- Psalm 119:105

PONDER & PRAY

Paul consistently urges Christians to show their love for one another. Take this verse from Philemon and rewrite it into your own prayer.

I am praying that you will really put your generosity to work, for in so doing you will come to an understanding of all the good things we can do for Christ. —Philemon 1:6, NLT

TRINKETS TO TREASURE

This week, your trinket will serve to remind you of your newest forays into Scripture application—a bottle of nail polish, with which you *apply* lustrous color to your nails. Each time you put on a fresh coat of polish, it can bring to mind your prayers through Bible passages. As you formulate each verse into a personal prayer, you are applying God's Word to your life. And His Word will begin to color your life in beautiful ways.

NOTES & PRAYER REQUESTS

CHAPTER EIGHT

PRAYING OUT LOUD

"[PETER] WENT TO THE HOME OF MARY, THE
MOTHER OF JOHN MARK. MANY PEOPLE WERE
GATHERED THERE, PRAYING."

Acts 12:12, NCV

*I*t's that time again. You can feel your pulse begin to race. You give your neighbor a nervous smile as chairs are pulled into a circle. Mouth dry, palms sweaty, eyes downcast, you prepare yourself for a time of mumbled phrases and awkward silences. It's . . . prayer meeting. The men are in another corner of the room, and you have joined the circle of women. You wait your turn, as the familiar lines work their way around the circle. "Bless him," "Help her," "Be with them." Your mind scrambles as the person two seats away takes the item you had thought to pray about. *Should* you pray out loud this week? You usually don't. There's a kind of unspoken understanding here—some are pray-ers, and some just aren't. You aren't. Your inner turmoil mounts as the woman on your right pauses significantly. After a quiet moment, the lady on your left takes up the baton and you breathe a sigh of relief.

CLEARING ↗ THE ↖ COBWEBS

Do you have somebody you regularly pray together with? How often do you pray?

1. Why is it so hard for some of us to pray out loud with other Christians?

2. If prayer is such a private thing, reserved for the seclusion of our prayer closets, then why do Christians spend so much time praying together? What does Jesus say in Matthew 18:19–20?

3. Jesus was often alone to pray, but He did pray *with* His disciples, too. Who does He gather around Himself for a prayer meeting in Luke 9:28?

> One of my favorite after-school games was "prayer meeting." The little parlor of our garage apartment became the St. John Missionary Baptist Church. The old sofa was the pew, and a tall-backed chair was the pulpit. Together, my Daddy Harrell and I sang old hymns and hollered out long-winded prayers. Those play prayer meetings were so engraved in my heart that I would transfer praying into a life-long activity and into the lives of my children and grandchildren.
>
> Thelma Wells

4. Zephaniah 2:1 declares, "Gather together and pray." There is power in uniting together with other believers in prayer. When Christians pray, God acts! Things happen. What happened in Acts 12:5–17?

5. Some people say prayer releases God's power. It's not that God cannot act upon His own initiative—He just likes to be asked! What was the result of united prayer in Acts 16:25–26?

Prayer isn't magic. Jesus did not come to make our suffering disappear in an instant. Instead He came to fill it with His presence.

Barbara Johnson

*P*rolonged prayer can be pretty dull at times. It calls to mind the droning of some dear elder, who intones a rambling invocation while the rest of the congregation shift from foot to foot, go through mental checklists, peek at their watches, and cover up great yawns. Face it, some people's prayers just put you to sleep!

But have you ever been to an organized evening of prayer—a concert of prayer? The leaders set an agenda, the people divide into small groups, and the time flies by as prayer and praise are intermingled. When you face your time of prayer, learn to implement these two elements of success. Go into your time of prayer with a plan of what to pray about, and intersperse your prayer requests with songs of praise. Time will slip by as you worship your Lord.

6. Nearly every prayer meeting you've ever attended has probably started the same way—with a call for prayer requests. By asking for prayer, we allow other Christians to see our needs. Even Paul had his prayer requests. What need does he bring before the Ephesian church in Ephesians 6:20?

7. Praying for one another's needs reminds us we are a community. When we are in our prayer closets, pouring out our hearts to God, we are focusing on just that—our needs. And this is good. But we are also a part of the body of Christ, and the concerns of the whole church should be our own. What does Ephesians 4:15–16 say about *our* union with other believers?

How often do we ignore God's rules for our lives because we're too busy, we're too involved in our own thing, we don't believe, we make up our own rules, or we choose to be downright rebellious? I can imagine God looking at us and saying, "My child, how many times does it take to convince you that My way is the right way? My timing is the perfect timing? My authority is the ultimate authority? My instructions will lead you to a way that has been designed for your good. Why don't you obey Me?" As He questions us, if we're sensitive to listen to His admonishment, we're quick to say "Father, I'm sorry!" Before the twinkling of an eye, He says, "Forgiven!"

Thelma Wells

8. Romans gives us another exhortation of Paul concerning our treatment of one another. What does he command in Romans 12:10?

9. During a prayer meeting, when people are invited to take turns leading in prayer, can a shy sister participate without actually opening her mouth?

DIGGING DEEPER

This week, instead of spending extra time searching out the Scriptures, spend a little extra time in prayer. Gather together a small group, whether it's the circle of sisters in your Bible study, your closest friends, your mom, or your children. Then, share your prayer requests and settle in for a time of sentence prayers. As you pray out loud together, don't allow yourself to become long-winded. Take turns offering up just one brief sentence in prayer. Each person in your group might touch on each prayer need by mentioning different facets of the situation. The united intercession moves rapidly around the room until it is completely blanketed in prayer.

PONDER & PRAY

The church in Colosse must have been searching for God's will for their lives. Make Paul's prayer here your own. Rewrite it in your own words.

So we have continued praying for you ever since we first heard about you. We ask God to give you a complete understanding of what He wants to do in your lives, and we ask Him to make you wise with spiritual wisdom. —Colossians 1:9, NLT

TRINKETS TO TREASURE

This week's little treasure is a reminder that all of us are a part of one another, especially when we are united in prayer. Knitting needles will call to mind the scripture in Ephesians which says we are "joined and knit together." As we join together in a prayer meeting, the threads of our prayers are woven together, knit into the blankets that cover, the nets that capture, and the ropes that bind. By uniting in prayer, God's power is unleashed.

NOTES & PRAYER REQUESTS

CHAPTER NINE

WARRIORS AND INTERCESSORS

"GOD KNOWS HOW OFTEN I PRAY FOR YOU. DAY AND NIGHT I BRING YOU AND YOUR NEEDS IN PRAYER TO GOD."

Romans 1:9, NLT

*I*t's printed on the backs of those postcards missionaries have printed up. It's listed on the bottom of signup sheets. We find it in church newsletters, on pledge cards, in the announcement section of our bulletins. It's at the bottom of every ministry needs checklist. It's the consolation prize for those who can't otherwise help. It's right after "I can commit to $10 a month for the Cady family serving in Spain" or under "I will provide eight dozen chocolate chip cookies for the youth bake sale." It's the line which says, "I will be praying."

How did prayer get jostled down to the bottom of the list? How did prayer become an afterthought? The answer to this is simple enough. It's just a matter of practicality. Christians are pretty giving people. They want to make a difference, and they like to be told what they can do to help. Most of us are very willing to provide a pan of brownies, save our soup labels, and donate a

CLEARING ↗ THE ↖ COBWEBS

Do you have something you love to do so much that you completely lose track of time? What is it?

package of diapers when it is needed. We like to roll up our sleeves or pull out our checkbooks, but it's *hard* to drop down onto our knees. Prayer just doesn't feel like we're *doing* enough.

1. What do you think of when I say "prayer warrior"? Well, I used to think it was a kind term for little old ladies in the church who were too old to be useful anymore. Too frail to change diapers, too tottering to corral a Sunday school class, too tired to serve coffee and doughnuts. But since nobody wanted these dear saints to feel left out, a big deal was made about the fact that they were praying. After all, *anyone* can pray! So what makes someone a prayer warrior?

> I've had times of intense prayer for my children. As a mother, I find solace in praying for my children during the good times and the bad. It's a fact, when our children are hurt or disappointed, confused or sad, we hurt too. I can't fix their hurt, but I can take it to the One who knows how to bring healing.
>
> Thelma Wells

2. One of the reasons we have a stereotype of old women as prayer warriors is because the Bible mentions some of these intercessors. Look up these passages. What sort of woman was able to dedicate herself to prayer?

Who is the famous widow in Luke 2:37 and how did she spend her time?

According to Acts 1:14, who would meet together constantly for prayer?

What was Paul's recommendation for a widow's occupation in 1 Timothy 5:5?

3. Though it may be hard for the *doers* among us to believe it, praying really is helping. There's proof of it! What does Paul say in 2 Corinthians 1:11?

4. Some women seem to have an extraordinary dedication to prayer. They have seen God act, and they are convinced of prayer's power. Do you know someone who is able to rely so completely on God? Have you had evidence of God's power in answer to your prayers?

5. Intercessors often have a unique perspective on life. Though they give of their hearts to pray for the needs of others, they have a clear grasp of the eternal. While they may lift up a prayer for Suzie's aunt's bout with cancer and Nancy's grandmother's upcoming surgery, they are also deeply concerned for the advancement of the kingdom. They wrestle with the unseen, and plead for God

> *We are urged to pray for one another, but that does not mean that we abdicate our individual commitment to pray for ourselves.*
>
> Sheila Walsh

to work in the lives of His people. What does Paul urge Christians to pray for in 2 Thessalonians 3:1? What does Jesus urge His followers to pray for in Matthew 9:38?

I have heard it said, the only people who should be pastors are those who could not be content doing anything else. Similarly, I have heard that the only people who should attempt to write poetry are those who cannot *not* write poetry. There's enough bad poetry out there to prove this point. Intercessors and prayer warriors are those Christians who cannot help but pray!

What about you? Can you not help but hug people? Can you not help but notice the emotions that people are trying desperately to hide? Can you not help but bake? Can you not help but draw, write letters, grow African violets, cuddle babies, make things look pretty, sing, read, organize, play piano, fix things, straighten pictures, take the lead, adopt stray animals, get someone to laugh? Only so much can be taught. God has gifted each of us uniquely with something we cannot help but do. What have you been given? Perfect pitch, an eye for color, a way with numbers, a knack for getting people to work together, a love for children, a recipe for a mean bowl of chili, a heart for animals? It may seem small, but given to God, it can accomplish much for His kingdom.

6. How does Jude describe our prayer in Jude 1:20?

Psalm 121:4 says, "Indeed He who watches over Israel will neither slumber nor sleep." It's consoling to know God not only doesn't sleep, but also He doesn't even get drowsy. We can depend on Him to attend to our every need twenty-four hours a day, seven days a week. That gives us peace.

Thelma Wells

7. Many prayer warriors will wake up in the middle of the night, feeling the urgency to take up some matter in prayer. David knew such seasons of prayer. How does he describe the nights he was having in Psalm 77:2–4?

8. Are you sitting there, thinking, "that is so not me"? Does this mean we don't have to pray as much if we aren't *gifted* as intercessors?

DIGGING DEEPER

Is God calling you to make a new commitment to prayer? Dedicate yourself to prayer on behalf of that person in your life who needs prayer the most—a rebellious teen, a struggling young mother, a pastor, a missionary, a college freshman, a hurting coworker. The Bible is filled with the call of God to men to commit themselves to Him, to devote themselves to His service. Here are a few verses that speak of this kind of dedication.

- Job 5:8
- Psalm 119:38
- Psalm 37:5
- 1 Corinthians 16:15

PONDER & PRAY

Paul prayed, and he kept on praying for his friends in the faith. Take this verse from Second Thessalonians and make Paul's prayer your own.

And so we keep on praying for you, that our God will make you worthy of the life to which he called you. And we pray that God, by his power, will fulfill all your good intentions and faithful deeds. —2 Thessalonians 1:11, NLT

TRINKETS TO TREASURE

Our intercessory treasure this week simply has to be a blanket. Whether we think we are gifted to be prayer warriors or not, we can certainly come to our Heavenly Father on someone else's behalf and simply blanket them with prayer. Night or day, when the Spirit brings someone to mind, send up prayers for them.

NOTES & PRAYER REQUESTS

CHAPTER TEN

THE ATTITUDE OF PRAYER

"YOUR ATTITUDE SHOULD BE THE SAME THAT CHRIST JESUS HAD."

Philippians 2:5, NLT

Are you in a rut with your "prayer tags"? To be sure, there is comfort in the familiarity of our addresses, but do you utter certain phrases without even thinking about what they mean anymore? I grew up in a "Dear Heavenly Father" kind of Christian circle, but have attended churches with both "Our Savior God" and "Father God" kinds of praying pastors. Our closing tags tend to fall into ruts as well. Are you a "Thy will be done," an "in Jesus' name," or a "for Your glory" kind of pray-er? If your prayer life seems a bit routine, why not put a little more thought into your openings and your closings. Show your Father in Heaven you are giving Him your full attention, not just rattling off a few phrases by rote. To be in an attitude of prayer, let God know you are really there!

CLEARING THE COBWEBS

Some folks call their Grandfather "Paw Paw" or "Gumpie," and their Grandmother "Grammy" or "Nana." The world is full of men who have been called "bud" and "boo," and women who have been known as "princess" and "pumpkin." Do you have special names for the people in your life—nicknames for those closest to you?

1. How would you describe the ambience of the last prayer meeting you attended?

> When we get away from the invasive noise and activity of this world that makes so many demands on our time and attention, when we tune into our relationship with Christ, we discover the wonder that we are waiting for. We can wait for wonder to come knocking at our door. But if we will be quiet and listen, we will hear it knocking at ours.
>
> Sheila Walsh

2. What words do you think the Lord would use to describe effective prayer? First Kings 8:30 gives us a couple of good examples.

3. The Lord places much value on the earnest prayer of one of His children. Paul urges believers to "continue earnestly in prayer" (Col. 4:2, NKJV). What does the Scripture say about prayer in James 5:16?

4. Does having an attitude of prayer mean the same thing as praying without ceasing?

or some of us, we are out of our comfort zones to even kneel at our bedsides. Yet what was the reaction of the men and women throughout the Bible who stood before their God? Moses removed his sandals and fell on his face before the burning bush. He also cowered in the cleft of the rock while the glory of God passed in front of him. Isaiah wailed, "I am undone!" as he prostrated himself before God's throne. Again and again, people have fallen on their faces, covered their heads, hidden their eyes, cried out for mercy, and wept in the presence of the Most Holy One.

5. The word "attitude" can also be used to describe the position of a person. For instance, we teach our children to bow their heads, fold their hands, and close their eyes when we pray. This is our most traditional attitude of prayer. How did folks in the Bible pray?

Ezra 10:1 _____

Psalm 77:2 _____

Mark 14:35 _____

John 3:8 _____

Acts 6:6 _____

Acts 9:40 _____

Acts 13:3 _____

Acts 20:36 _____

1 Timothy 2:8 _____

6. Why do we kneel in prayer? Why do we raise our hands? Why do we bow our heads in the presence of the Lord?

I believe one of the best ways to get in a praying mood is to listen to music that ushers you into a spirit of adoration. That, in turn, takes your mind off the problem you are facing and helps you to focus on the Problem Solver. It brings harmony to your soul.

Thelma Wells

7. You've heard the story of the rebellious youngster who, when forced to take a seat on the stool in the corner, announced to his mother that he was still standing up on the inside. Though our heads are bowed, hands folded, and eyes closed, what needs to be going on inside? What is an inward attitude of prayer?

> *Over the last few years I have discovered that what is most changed by prayer is the one who is praying. I see that prayer changes me. I can't stay the same when I pray. I start with one stance, but as I spend time with God looking at the situation, I find that the world shifts a little. I'm given new perspective on what I see.*
>
> Sheila Walsh

8. So often our prayers echo those of the psalmist. We call to God, knowing He will give us His attention. What is David's request in Psalm 17:1?

9. Our Father always hears our prayers—and gives us His attention. But do we reciprocate in this? Do we listen to the Lord, paying attention to His words to us? Consider the prophet's lament in Isaiah 30:9. How are those who do not listen to God's instructions described?

DIGGING DEEPER

Earnest prayers are featured throughout the pages of the Bible. Look up these few, and see how God honored them.

- Mark 5:23   • Luke 7:4   • Luke 22:44   • James 5:17

PONDER & PRAY

Paul was able to encompass so much of life in just a few words of prayer. This brief prayer in Romans serves to encourage our hearts. Rewrite it as a prayer of your own—make it fit your life today.

So I pray that God, who gives you hope, will keep you happy and full of peace as you believe in him. May you overflow with hope through the power of the Holy Spirit.—Romans 15:13, NLT

TRINKETS TO TREASURE

James, the brother of Jesus, knew a thing or two about prayer. He is the one who wrote, "the effective, fervent prayer of a righteous man avails much" (James 5:17, NKJV). This James spent so much time on his knees in prayer, he came to be nicknamed "Old Camel Knees." So our trinket for this week, to remind us to continue in an attitude of earnest prayer, is a camel.

NOTES & PRAYER REQUESTS

CHAPTER ELEVEN

How He Answers

"When I pray, you answer me; You encourage me by giving me the strength I need."

Psalm 138:3, NLT

We pray. We tell God all our concerns. We make requests on behalf of our loved ones. We send our heart's cry right into His throne room. And then, we must wait. No confirmation that a message has been received. No receipts. No quick answers.

When we have questions, we really like to get answers. It's a system we're accustomed to. Even when we cannot get in touch with someone immediately, we have options. We leave our name and number on answering machines. We leave messages on others' voice mail services. We can even get confirmation that our e-mail messages have been received. We know they'll get back to us at their earliest convenience.

But God doesn't make any such promise to us. Sometimes, the answer comes before we can even finish praying. Sometimes, a door closes with such a resounding thud that we know the answer must be no. But more often than not, God makes us wait.

CLEARING ⚐ THE ⚐ COBWEBS

What is the strangest answering machine message you've ever heard?

69

1. One of the comforts of prayer is, we know, no matter what the answer might be, that in His own time, God *will* answer. David knew this. What did he say in Psalm 17:6?

> One of my physical responses to the poison still working its way out of my system has been hair loss. I was rather embarrassed to bring it up to God, but when I prayed my hair prayer, there was the immediate inner assurance that hair would indeed come, for the purpose of Marilyn "knowing" that God is God. The hair came! I cannot even begin to understand or explain the divine "why" of my hair experience. The hair is merely something visible that God is using tangibly to assure me of His divine power, His sovereign design to raise me up again in spite of how I felt or even look, and the outlandish lengths to which He'll go to reassure me of His love and power.
>
> Marilyn Meberg

2. There are times when God answers our prayers with amazing speed. Daniel had an example of this in his life. Read Daniel 9:21–23. Why does Gabriel say he has come?

3. The prayers God answers are often everyday prayers, still miraculous in their own way. What prayer does God answer in Psalm 34:4?

4. What kinds of prayers can God answer? Jesus answers this for us in Mark 11:24.

5. There is another example of answered prayer given by Paul in Philippians 1:19. What does he declare?

*U*sually, when we pray, we know exactly what we want God to do. We've given our situation much thought, we've checked out the pros and cons, considered our options, and we've decided how God should work. As we kneel in prayer, we unfold carefully laid plans, hoping for His stamp of approval. Once we get the nod from on high, we can move forward smoothly with life.

Unfortunately, God doesn't operate this way. I think He delights in surprising us. Just look at all the surprises He slipped into the Bible! Sarah had a baby when she was ninety-nine years old. Jacob was reunited with the son he thought had been killed by wild animals. The eighth boy in a family of shepherds from Bethlehem is sought out by God's prophet and anointed as the next king of Israel. The widow who shared the last bit of food in her house with Elijah found herself in possession of a pitcher that never ran out of oil. A poor, orphaned Jewish girl becomes the Queen of Persia and saves her people from a murderous plot. The man thrown into a den of hungry lions comes out alive the next day and receives a promotion instead. Improbable? Unbelievable? Incredible? Inconceivable? And yet, true.

Things don't always work out the way we think they should. But sometimes that's because God has something better in mind.

6. When I was little, I knew when my mom said, "No," it meant no. "Maybe" usually meant yes. "I'll think about it" most often meant no. And "We'll see" generally meant yes. There are times, when God will tell us "No." He doesn't always give us what we want. Have you ever experienced a "No" from God that you were grateful to have received in hindsight?

Are you dealing with someone whom you feel will never change? Do you vacillate between wishing he would change and just wanting him to leave you alone? Have you given up expecting good things from that person? Nobody is so far from God that he can't get back to the Lord. Our responsibility is to keep knocking at God's door about that person, to keep believing God will answer our prayers. Thank God for what He will do. Patiently but expectantly wait on the Lord. Renew your hope!

Thelma Wells

7. Of all the answers my parents ever gave to my questions, the hardest to live with was "Wait and see." It was enough to make an impatient child squirm with frustration. Does God make us wait? Yep. How does David encourage us to handle ourselves while we wait in Psalm 27:14?

8. Psalm 130:5 says, "I wait for the Lord, my soul waits, And in His word I do hope" (NKJV). So, while we await the answers we seek through prayer, we can gather hope from God's Word. What promise does God give to those who are waiting in Isaiah 40:31?

9. Micah felt sure God would answer him, "Therefore I will look to the Lord; I will wait for the God of my salvation; My God will hear me" (Mic. 7:7, NKJV). But what do we do in the meantime? What should be our manner—our behavior—as we await God's answer to our prayers? Look at David's urging in Psalm 62:5.

> *My husband died at age fifty-two of cancer; our baby died when she was two weeks old; scores of people prayed, but God did not choose to do what I longed for. Why not? God simply does what He does because He's God. I'll never figure Him out.*
>
> Marilyn Meberg

10. Even when we know the answers we seek will come eventually, waiting can be hard. So here is one last verse of encouragement from the prophet Jeremiah. Look up Lamentations 3:25–26. What is God's promise to those who seek Him?

Digging Deeper

God can answer our prayers for us even as we are asking Him. Here are a couple of stories from our Bibles where God did just that!

- Genesis 24:15   • Acts 9:11

PONDER & PRAY

The prayers Paul wrote in His letters are the very same prayers we can and should be praying for one another. Lift this one up on your own behalf by rewriting it here.

May you always be filled with the fruit of your salvation—those good things that are produced in your life by Jesus Christ—for this will bring much glory and praise to God.—Philippians 1:11, NLT

TRINKETS TO TREASURE

Your little bit of a treasure this week is a seed—a bundle of potential, just waiting to be planted. It will remind you that when you pray, it is like planting a seed. God's answer will come, just like the flowers will eventually come up from the earth. But we must be patient, waiting for the proper time, until we can enjoy the color and fragrance of the first blossom. Don't become discouraged if God seems slow to answer your heart's cry. Keep on praying, and planting, and someday there may be a whole garden blooming to His glory.

Notes & Prayer Requests

CHAPTER TWELVE

SAYING THANK YOU

"CONTINUE EARNESTLY IN PRAYER, BEING VIGILANT IN IT WITH THANKSGIVING."

Colossians 4:2, NKJV

o you know what a Thanksgiving go-around is? It's the special time on Thanksgiving day, when you're all gathered around the table. The turkey is golden brown, the butter is melting over the bowl of mashed potatoes, the vegetables are steaming, and the gelatin mold is glistening. Then, before you can dig in, Mom calls for a go-around. Everybody at the table must quickly come up with a reason to be grateful. "What are you most thankful for this year?" The usual answers are offered up: family, house, health, job, friends, a chance to rest over the long weekend. With young children, however, the answers can be rather humorous. Over the years, my daughter has given thanks for every- thing from her favorite baby doll to snow. And my son almost always answers that he is most thank- ful for mashed potatoes and gravy.

We may roll our eyes, and consider their answers childish and petty. But wait! How won- derful to be thankful for the very thing in front of you. Their prayers may be simple, but they are

CLEARING THE COBWEBS

Name one thing you have, until this moment of consideration, taken completely for granted.

honest. Learning to appreciate God's many blessings will lend a richness to your prayer life. Don't neglect to tell Him you've noticed all His good gifts.

1. For what are you most thankful today? What would you thank God for right now?

2. We could not do a thing without our Lord Jesus as the source of our salvation, our strength, and our service. How does Paul put it in 1 Timothy 1:12?

> *Each day I thank God that I can eat, drink, get dressed, seek to do His will, now. And then I pray the most powerful prayer: "Lord, close the doors I don't need to walk through today. Open the doors I do. Steer me away from people I don't need to deal with today. Put people in my path that I do. And, Lord, don't let me waste time."*
>
> Thelma Wells

3. So, our prayers must ever hold an element of gratitude. What does Paul most often give thanks for in his letters? Ephesians 1:16 says so. Philemon 1:4 also gives a good example.

4. Learning to be thankful is a part of our Christian experience. Sometimes we are so consumed by our troubles, we forget to be thankful for the things right in front of us. What does James 5:13 say?

5. Did you ever feel so happy you wished you had the voice of Sheila Walsh, so you could sing it to the world? The Scriptures often equate a heart overflowing with thanksgiving to songs of praise. Look at these verses. How does singing give voice to a grateful heart?

Psalm 69:30 _____

Psalm 95:2 _____

Psalm 147:7 _____

Isaiah 51:3 _____

How are you about sending thank you notes? Apparently, these courtesies are supposed to be mailed off no more than three days after the receipt of a gift or the date of a dinner party. The only ones afforded a grace period are new brides, who are given three months to complete their task.

Have you been putting off sending thank you notes to God? Do you take His blessings for granted? Have you told God how much you appreciate Him? Why not consider starting a Thank You Book. It doesn't have to be fancy—a notebook would do. It won't take more than a few moments each day. It's your chance to "Count Your Blessings." Every day, write down one thing you are thankful for. The only rule is, you may never duplicate your item. Think of something new each day. Trust me, you'll never run out of things to say, even if you are thanking God for the things right in front of you—strawberries, the inventor of toothpaste, the story of Jonah, sunsets, washing machines, photocopiers, parmesan cheese, terry cloth. Make a Thank You Book a part of your daily quiet time with the Lord.

6. Does your Sunday school class or prayer circle take time at the beginning of each meeting to share prayer requests? Of course, we are accustomed to this. Do you also consider it an opportunity to share matters of thanksgiving—praises from the week just spent? What does David say in Psalm 26:7 about sharing our praises?

> Whether our "Thank yous" are momentary, intentional pauses in the midst of a hectic day, thank-you notes to God for His many blessings, or lengthy discourses of His grace, cultivating an attitude of gratitude will remind us of the truth that undergirds our lives: "For the Lord is good and His love endures forever; His faithfulness continues through all generations" (Ps. 100:5).
>
> Sheila Walsh

7. What's another reason that sharing our praises is a good thing? Second Corinthians 4:15 gives us an excellent reason. What is it?

8. Psalm 107:22 declares, "Let them sacrifice the sacrifices of thanksgiving. And declare His works with rejoicing." Why do you suppose the psalmist refers to his prayers of thanksgiving as sacrifices of praise?

9. A heart of thanksgiving is essential to our faith. How does Paul put it in Colossians 2:7?

10. How long will we be praying? How long will our thanksgiving rise up before the throne? Read Revelation 7:12 to see.

DIGGING DEEPER

In the Book of Nehemiah, there is a fascinating story of how the children of Israel, long separated from their temple and its traditions, rediscover the worship of God. A large portion of Nehemiah, chapter 12, details the uncovering of the psalms of thanksgiving written by David and the establishment of two large thanksgiving choirs to sing during a worship service. To read more about it, read Nehemiah 12.

For in the days of David and Asaph of old there were chiefs of the singers, and songs of praise and thanksgiving to God. —Nehemiah 12:46, NKJV

PONDER & PRAY

Here is one last prayer from Paul to serve as our benediction. Using your own words, make his prayer your own.

May you experience the love of Christ, though it is so great you will never fully understand it. Then you will be filled with the fullness of life and power that comes from God. —Ephesians 3:19, NLT

81

Trinkets to Treasure

Your trinket for this week is a thank you note. It is a reminder to fill your prayer life with notes of praise. God welcomes our conversational prayers, our prayers of personal petition, our prayers of intercession for others. But God treasures our prayers of thanksgiving. Show the Lord how much you appreciate what He has done for you—that you have noticed His hand in your day, and that you love Him for it.

Notes & Prayer Requests

SHALL WE REVIEW?

Every chapter has added a new trinket to your treasure trove of memories. Let's remind ourselves of the lessons they hold for us!

1. An Invitation

God has invited you to come to Him in prayer. He wants you to call upon Him, so set your mind on Him and pour out your heart.

2. A Brass Button

A reminder that we have been given the right to come boldly before God's throne in prayer—bold as brass. Though our Heavenly Father demands respect, we are welcomed as His own child.

3. A Recipe Card

Print the Lord's Prayer on it to remind yourself of Christ's example, but then play with the recipe every time you pray, using your creativity and making it your own.

4. Earplugs

Everyone needs a prayer closet—a place reserved for prayer. Even in the midst of the busiest households, we can find a tiny pool of peace when we turn our thoughts to God.

5. A Cork

A teasing reminder to "put a cork in it" and spend some of our prayer time listening to our Lord. Listen for His leading as you soak yourself in the Scriptures.

6. A Journal

A blank book for you to fill. Let it stand as a record of God's faithfulness to you. A place for meditation and application. A testament to your spiritual walk.

7. Nail Polish

As you begin the practice of praying through Scripture passages, a bottle of polish serves to remind you of how you can apply the Scriptures to your life.

8. Knitting Needles

We pray for one another because we are "joined and knit together." Because we are all a part of one another in the body of Christ, we pray out loud together, remembering one another's needs.

9. A Blanket

God may be calling you to be an intercessor—a prayer warrior—on behalf of someone dear to you. Night and day, your prayers will blanket them.

10. A Camel

With a nod to James, the brother of Jesus, who was nicknamed "Old Camel Knees," we remember we should continue through our days in an attitude of prayer.

11. A Seed

Each prayer we send up is like a seed, filled with potential. Yet God answers in His own way and in His own time, just as a seed takes time and care to germinate, grow, and flower. When we pray, we must simply trust that God will answer.

12. A Thank You Note

A reminder to fill your prayer life with notes of praise. Show the Lord how much you appreciate what He has done for you—that you have noticed His hand in your day, and that you love Him for His care.

LEADER'S GUIDE

Chapter 1

1. "Call upon Me in the day of trouble; I will deliver you, and you shall glorify Me" (Ps. 50:15, NKJV). God's message is clear: if you are in trouble, call for Him. He will help you. Interestingly enough, God even tells us why He will hear and rescue us. It is for His glory. Since giving God glory should be the goal of our lives, we find in this verse the silver lining to every dark cloud we may encounter in this life. Even in our most desperate circumstances, we can glorify God simply by calling out to Him.

2. "Remember, never pray to or swear by any other gods. Do not even mention their names" (Ex. 23:13, NLT). God wants to have a relationship with you, but He's very concerned that this be an exclusive relationship! God must be your one and only when it comes to praise and prayer.

3. "Listen to my cry for help, my King and my God, for I will never pray to anyone but you" (Ps. 5:2, NLT). Honor God in your heart by making Him the first one you turn to, whether you are sharing your turmoil, your sorrows, your stresses, your suffering, your disappointments, your frustrations—or your triumphs, your thankfulness, your joy, your excitement, your success, or your contentment.

4. "Then men began to call on the name of the Lord" (Gen. 4:26, NKJV). People began to pray.

5. If you truly believe something, your actions will prove it. What you believe affects your choices, decisions, actions. Are you neglecting your prayer life? Is God still waiting for you to turn towards Him and share your heart? Make your first prayer one for faith! Ask God to bolster your belief so prayer can begin to flow to your Father.

6. "I am praying to you because I know you will answer, O God. Bend down and listen as I pray" (Ps. 17:6, NLT). It would be pointless to pray to a god who could do nothing. It would be foolish to pray to a god who could not hear your words. David shows some logic, and a bit of common sense here, in praising God for His ability to answer.

7. "Through each day the Lord pours His unfailing love upon me, and through each night I sing His songs, praying to God who gives me life" (Ps. 42:8, NLT). God gives us life. God pours out His love on us. God is unfailing. Such blessings were enough to inspire David's rich prayer life, and the composition of the many psalms—his songs—that he put to music and sang in worship.

8. "Because He has inclined His ear to me, therefore I will call upon Him as long as I live" (Ps. 116:2, NKJV). God's faithfulness has given a firm foundation for faith. Trust is built, and the psalmist pledges lifelong loyalty to God. For as long as he has breath, God will receive his prayers and his praise.

Chapter 2

1. We know from the Gospels that God is our Father, who loves us, provides for us, and has made a way for our salvation. When we consider these things, it is easy to understand God is Love, and our hearts respond to His call. Yet God is unchanging, and so the same Heavenly Father we pray to now is just as much the God of the Old Testament. In His presence, men fell—crumpling in the dirt, cowering in fear, hiding their faces. God is sinless, just, and jealous. This is a God we dare not cross. He is to be acknowledged, obeyed, and given proper respect. So, necessarily, our prayers are a blend of the familiarity of friendship, and respect for the Divine.

2. "Let the earth fear the Lord; let all the inhabitants of the world stand in awe of Him" (Ps. 33:8, NKJV). Scripture tells us of the awe and fearful respect that He is due. In fact, throughout the Old Testament, God's followers are not called "believers" or "Christians" or "disciples" as they are now. Instead, those who live in obedience to God were called a people who feared God. The only people who did not fear God were those who did not know about Him!

3. "You believe there is one God. Good! But the demons believe that, too, and they tremble with fear" (James 2:19, NCV). Though it may be grudging, even the demons have a healthy respect for our Heavenly Father. The very thought of Him sets their knees to knocking.

4. "And now, Israel, what does the Lord your God require of you, but to fear the Lord your God, to walk in all His ways and to love Him, to serve the Lord your God with all your heart and with all your soul" (Deut. 10:12, NKJV). This fear—a mingling of respect, obedience, awe, love, and loyalty—should remain in our hearts as well!

5. "I prayed, 'O my God, I am utterly ashamed; I blush to lift up my face to you. For our sins are piled higher than our heads, and our guilt has reached to the heavens'" (Ezra 9:6, NLT). Those who rightly fear God have a good grasp on the reality of sin. Ezra came to God, but he needed to begin with confession.

6. "Turn from your wickedness and pray to the Lord. Perhaps He will forgive your evil thoughts" (Acts 8:22, NLT). We must confess our sins to our Father. We must ask for His forgiveness. We must turn from sin.

7. Second Chronicles 7:14 lays out God's expectations for contrite hearts: "If my people who are called by my name will humble themselves and pray and seek my face and turn from their wicked ways, I will hear from heaven and will forgive their sins and heal their land" (NKJV). The pattern is simple: humbling, praying, seeking, and turning. In response to such an earnest confession, God promises to listen. As it says in 1 Kings 8:30, "Hear in heaven Your dwelling place; and when You hear, forgive" (NKJV).

8. "Let us therefore come boldly to the throne of grace, that we may obtain mercy and find grace to help in time of need" (Heb. 4:16, NKJV). God has promised to give us His mercy, His grace, and the help we need. These are the kinds of things we are welcome to bring before His throne, and these are the kinds of things God has promised to provide.

9. You can come to God with boldness because He has given you every reason to do so. He has removed your sins (Ps. 103:12). He has clothed you in righteousness (Ps. 32:1). He has adopted you into His own family, calling you His child (Rom. 8:15). He has also called you His friend (John 15:15). Jesus is your advocate, praying even now on your behalf (Heb. 7:25). And the Spirit is helping you to pray, even when you aren't sure what to say (Rom. 8:26). With all these assurances, why not be bold!

Chapter 3

2. "The Pharisee stood and prayed thus with himself, 'God, I thank You that I am not like other men—extortioners, unjust, adulterers, or even as this tax collector. I fast twice a week; I give tithes of all that I possess'" (Luke 18:11–12, NKJV). The Pharisee seems to be commending himself to heaven—listing his accomplishments and polishing up his assets. He compares himself to "worse" sinners, and gloats over his superiority to them. But the Pharisee's prayer never even reaches heaven. Jesus even makes the point of saying he "prayed thus with himself." In contrast, the tax collector comes before God, sorrowing over his sins. Ashamed, he doesn't lift his eyes. Humbled, he drops to his knees and beats his chest. Here is a man who knows he has sinned, knows he is unworthy, and knows he needs mercy. This is the man who is forgiven.

3. "When you pray, don't babble on and on as people of other religions do. They think their prayers are answered only by repeating their words again and again" (Matt. 6:7). This is not to say that persistent prayer is a no-no. When our hearts are heavy over some matter, we can continue to bring it before the Lord in prayer. Even Jesus prayed about the same things over and over (Matt. 26:44). It is the mindless prattling, and the superstitious belief that the words of the prayer themselves are powerful which brings a reprimand from our Lord. There is nothing magical in chanting some phrase that will ensure God's response to your prayer.

4. The matching should line up like so: g, k, d, a, f, h, e, l, c, b, j, and i.

5. "God knows how often I pray for you. Day and night I bring you and your needs in prayer to God" (Rom. 1:9, NLT). The letters of Paul are filled with such encouragements. "They will pray for you with deep affection because of the wonderful grace of God shown through you" (2 Cor. 9:14, NLT). He let his friends know they were in his heart and in his prayers—"night and day praying exceedingly that we may see your face and perfect what is lacking in your faith" (1 Thess. 3:10, NKJV).

6. Colossians 4:4 gives the request, "Pray that I will proclaim this message as clearly as I should" (NLT). Take time each week to pray for your pastor—for his wisdom, his words, and his weekly message. 1 Timothy 2:1 brings us to our knees for all of the non-believers of the world: "I urge you, first of all, to pray for all people. As you make your requests, plead for God's mercy upon them" (NLT). And Colossians 4:3 offers a plea for the opportunity to tell others about Jesus: "Praying for us, that God would open to us a door for the word, to speak the mystery of Christ" (NKJV).

7. "Don't worry about anything; instead, pray about everything. Tell God what you need, and thank Him for all He has done" (Phil. 4:6, NLT). Nothing is too insignificant for God. Nothing is beneath His interest. He welcomes you to bring everything to Him.

8. "The Holy Spirit helps us in our distress. For we don't even know what we should pray for, nor how we should pray. But the Holy Spirit prays for us with groanings that cannot be expressed in words" (Rom. 8:26, NLT). The Spirit comes alongside, and communicates to the Father for us, giving utterance to the groaning of our hearts.

9. "I say to you, though he will not rise and give to him because he is his friend, yet because of his persistence he will rise and give him as many as he needs" (Luke 11:8, NKJV). According to Jesus, persistence gets results.

10. Jesus promises answers. Ask, and you will get an answer. Seek, and you will find what you need. Knock, and the doors will open before you. What's more, Jesus gives us an assurance that we will not be unpleasantly surprised by God's answers. God knows how to give good gifts to His children. And Jesus tells His disciples here the first gift will be the best of all—the Holy Spirit.

Chapter 4

1. Though our prayers will be heard no matter when or where we whisper them, having a regular time of private prayer each day is so important. Do you value your relationship with your Savior enough to put Him into your schedule? Does your busy day include a timeslot blocked off just for Him? Give God the highest priority. Give Him your time and attention. He will reward you greatly for it.

2. Here are some brief descriptions of the prayer habits of these faithful followers of God: Daniel 6:10—Daniel would go to an upstairs window in his home—the one that faced towards Jerusalem—and kneel to pray three times every day. Mark 1:35—Jesus would get up very early in the morning and go for a walk in the countryside to pray. Luke 6:12—Jesus would sometimes go up into the mountains to pray, and His prayer vigils could extend right on through the night. Acts 10:2—Cornelius was a devout man, given to regular times of prayer to God, even though he was a Gentile. Acts 16:25—Paul and Silas were up until midnight, mingling their urgent prayers to God with songs of praise. 1 Thessalonians 3:10—Paul and his companions came together in prayer for their many friends in the faith day and night.

3. "May these words that I have prayed in the presence of the Lord be before Him constantly, day and night" (1 Kin. 8:59, NLT). Solomon wanted the words of his prayer to linger on in the ears of God. He didn't want God to forget what he'd pleaded for, as king of God's people. He was trusting God to uphold His own people, and provide for their daily needs. Solomon wanted his prayer to be constantly before God, an ongoing call for His aid and protection.

4. "Pray at all times and on every occasion in the power of the Holy Spirit. Stay alert and be persistent in your prayers for all Christians everywhere" (Eph. 6:18, NLT). According to Paul, prayer should be Spirit-led, persistent, all-encompassing, and constant.

5. Do you have a family member who doesn't know Jesus? Are you on your knees for a rebellious child? Are you dedicating yourself to prayer for a missionary who is serving overseas? Does your Sunday school class generate a prayer list every week so you can be lifting each other up in prayer? Who does God bring to your mind whenever you pray—your neighbors, your daughter's roommate at college, the nice man at the post office, the young girl who serves tables at your favorite restaurant, the coworker who is going through a messy divorce, the boy who delivers your newspapers?

6. Those who wanted to find God found a place in which to pray. Here are the examples we found in the Bible: Jonah 2:1—Jonah was very alone in the fish's belly! Don't wait so long to get alone with God that He needs to use such drastic measures to get your attention! **Matthew 14:23**—Jesus sent the crowds away so He could be alone. **Mark 6:46**—Jesus went into the hills by Himself. **Luke 5:16**—Jesus withdrew into the wilderness to pray. **Luke 18:10**—The Jews would go to the Temple in order to pray. **Luke 22:41**—Jesus went a short distance from the others to be alone. **Acts 10:9**—Peter spent some time in prayer up on the rooftop patio. **Revelation 1:9–10**—John took some time away from prison life to spend his Sunday in prayer.

7. Some of us have a favorite chair. Some of us pray while we wash our hair in the shower. Some of us make use of a long commute to communicate with God. Is it at the kitchen table, where you sip your first cup of coffee every morning? Is it in your office, before the routine of the day begins? Is it under the covers of your bed, before you drift off to sleep each night, or before you rise up in the morning? Though God is always with us, no matter where we are, we are creatures of habit. When we establish a meeting place with God, He draws us there, waits for us there, touches us there. He honors our choice of time and place, and He keeps the appointment faithfully.

8. "And when you pray, you shall not be like the hypocrites. For they love to pray standing in the synagogues and on the corners of the streets, that they may be seen by men. Assuredly, I say to you, they have their reward" (Matt. 6:5, NKJV). The hypocrite prays in order to call attention to himself. He purposely seeks out the spotlight, standing where many people will notice his righteousness, craving the admiration of other men. God does not hear his prayers.

9. Do hypocrites get a reward? You bet they do! But it isn't one which will last. They trade God's listening ear for the attention of men. They trade God's blessing for the good opinion of their neighbors. They trade God's glory for the admiration of their friends. And sometimes, we are a little jealous of all the attention they receive. Do you sometimes want to call attention to your faithfulness too? Are you occasionally tempted to point out your own devotion? Jesus warns us not to fall into this trap.

10. "But you, when you pray, go into your room, and when you have shut your door, pray to your Father who is in the secret place; and your Father who sees in secret will reward you openly" (Matt. 6:6, NKJV). When it comes to your personal relationship with God, prayer is a private matter. You don't need to tell others about it, or prove yourself, or explain yourself to anyone else. With God you can be your most vulnerable, your most honest, your most private. Keep your trysts with Him in a precious, secret place. You may never be acclaimed as a prayer warrior in your church, or receive special respect from others in your congregation, but it doesn't matter. Jesus' promise is clear. Your Father will make sure your faithfulness is rewarded.

Chapter 5

1. "And they belong to the world, so what they say is from the world, and the world listens to them. But we belong to God, and those who know God listen to us. But those who are not from God do not listen to us. That is how we know the Spirit that is true and the spirit that is false" (1 John 4:5–6, NCV). If you are not keeping your ear tuned to your Father's leading, then you leave yourself open to the very persuasive influences of the world.

2. "For as many as are led by the Spirit of God, these are sons of God" (Rom. 8:14, NKJV). Very few people will try to tell you that God speaks to them in an audible voice. But the Holy Spirit which indwells us is an effective communicator. Call it what you will—urging, influencing, prompting, leading, drawing, impressing, compelling—the Spirit lets us know when we should or shouldn't be doing something.

3. "Faith comes by hearing, and hearing by the word of God" (Rom. 10:17, NKJV). There's a very good reason that a time of personal devotion—

one's quiet time—consists of prayer and Scripture reading. Therein lie the two elements of conversation with God: talking to God and listening to His Word.

4. The Bible is not an ordinary book. God's Word is not some outdated antiquity. Hebrews 4:12 declares, "The word of God is living and powerful, and sharper than any two-edged sword . . . and is a discerner of the thoughts and intents of the heart" (NKJV). The truth of the Scriptures uncovers our hearts, convicts us of sin, and shows us the path to redemption. Jesus said, "Man shall not live by bread alone, but by every word of God" (Luke 4:4, NKJV). We could not live without God's Word any more than our bodies could live without food. Though we might spend our entire lifetimes plumbing the depths of the Scriptures, we will always discover something new our Heavenly Father wants to teach us. In our conversations with God, *He* takes the lead. He has already spoken. We are merely picking up the thread when we read His Word. Prayer is our response to Him.

5. "For this reason we also thank God without ceasing, because when you received the word of God which you heard from us, you welcomed it not as the word of men, but as it is in truth, the word of God, which also effectively works in you who believe" (1 Thess. 2:13, NKJV). God's Word—our Bibles—are truth. And when we spend time reading, absorbing, and being influenced by God's true words, we are effectively changed by it.

6. David in Psalm 102:18—"This will be written for the generation to come, that a people yet to be created may praise the Lord" (NKJV). John in John 20:31—"These are written that you may believe that Jesus is the Christ, the Son of God, and that believing you may have life in His name" (NKJV). Paul in Romans 15:4—"For whatever things were written before were written for our learning, that we through the patience and comfort of the Scriptures might have hope" (NKJV). John again in 1 John 5:13—"These things I have written to you who believe in the name of the Son of God, that you may know that you have eternal life, and that you may continue to believe in the name of the Son of God" (NKJV). God's Word was preserved for us so we too would praise God, so we would believe in Jesus Christ, so we could have eternal life, and to give us hope.

7. "Study this Book of the Law continually. Meditate on it day and night so you may be sure to obey all that is written in it. Only then will you succeed" (Josh. 1:8, NLT). The same holds true for each of us as well.

8. No wonder the Word of God is living. No wonder the Word of God is powerful. No wonder it is eternal. According to Revelation 19:13, "His name is called The Word of God" (NKJV). Jesus is Himself the Living Word.

Chapter 6

1. When we write something down, we are less likely to forget it.

2. **Psalm 63:6**—We can meditate in bed, throughout the night. **Psalm 77:12**—We can meditate on the things that God has done in our lives, or throughout the pages of our Bibles. **Psalm 119:48**—We can meditate on God's commandments, becoming so familiar with them that we love them. **Psalm 119:148**—Sometimes, God wakes us in the night, just so we have a chance to meditate over His Word and works. **Psalm 143:5**—We meditate on God's care of us in the past, and on the beauty of His creation in which we have a special place.

3. "Finally brethren whatever things are true, whatever things are noble, whatever things are just, whatever things are pure, whatever things are lovely, whatever things are of good report, if there is any virtue and if there is anything praiseworthy—meditate on these things" (Phil. 4:8, NKJV). Does the activity of your spare time fit into this criteria? Before you pick up a book, flip through a magazine, pop in an audio tape, or turn on your television, consider these words of Paul. Perhaps turning to your prayer closet, your Bible, and your prayer journal would be more pleasing to your Lord.

4. Progress. "Meditate on these things; give yourself entirely to them, that your progress may be evident to all" (1 Tim. 4:15, NKJV). When we focus our attention on our relationship with God, His input in our lives, His will for our daily walk, on continued prayer, and on written meditation—we grow. God changes us, and we will mature and bear fruit for His glory.

5. Paul asks Timothy to serve as a pattern of blameless living for his fellow Christians. He should be loving, pure, and strong in his faith. Paul tells Timothy to use his spiritual gifts. He is to meditate, making his spiritual life the focus of his days. Paul urges Timothy to keep his guard up, checking both himself and his teaching to make sure he is remaining true to the Lord. Such should be our prayer as well.

6. "My God! Now I am deeply discouraged, but I will remember your kindness" (Ps. 42:6, NKJV). Pondering God's hand in our lives as we look over His days, months, and years of care, deepens our trust in His continued faithfulness.

7. Though it may not seem quite reverent to write in your *Holy* Bible, it really is okay. What is the purpose of reading after all? As we read and reread the Scriptures, our notes help to remind us the lessons we have learned before. Repetition is a good teacher.

8. For some of us, prayer puts us in a place as familiar and comfortable as an old shoe. Peace and joy are our companions. For others of us, the familiarity described sounds wonderful. Our hearts long for such a nearness, such a friendship, but we cannot honestly say we have ever experienced it. Perhaps even now, the Lord is calling you to take up a pen and begin to record the journey to His side as you seek Him.

9. "Repeat them again and again to your children. Talk about them when you are at home and when you are away on a journey, when you are lying down and when you are getting up again" (Deut. 6:7, NLT). The story of your growing experience, of God's faithfulness to you, and of the prayers He has answered, may be an inspiration to your closest friends and family when you are gone.

10. "When I pray, you answer me; you encourage me by giving me the strength I need" (Ps. 138:3, NLT). As you consider the answers you have seen, and the unexpected ways in which God has worked in your life, you can be encouraged to keep praying.

Chapter 7

There are no wrong answers here! Going through the five Scriptures listed, encourage the members of your group to share what they learned as they meditated and prayed through those Scriptures. Encourage them and discuss their insights as a group.

Chapter 8

1. It's speech class all over again—stage fright. Also, we don't always know what to say, how to say it, or the right words to use.

2. "Again I say to you that if two of you agree on earth concerning anything that they ask, it will be done for them by My Father in heaven. For where two or three are gathered together in My name, I am there in the midst of them" (Matt. 18:19–20). Though we have a personal relationship with our Savior, and our relationship with Him is cultivated in the privacy of our prayer closets, Christianity is not for hermits. We are a congregation, a community, a body of believers. It is through our love for one another that the world can see the love of God. In a similar way, our prayers, when joined with those of our sisters, reach our Lord and urge Him to answer.

3. "Jesus took Peter, James, and went up on a mountain to pray" (Luke 9:28, NKJV). Though the twelve traveled with Him everywhere, Jesus seems to have taken Peter, James, and John into His special confidence. These three were closest to Him, and He prayed together with them on occasion.

4. "Peter was therefore kept in prison, but constant prayer was offered to God for him by the church" (Acts 12:5, NKJV). The Christian church in Jerusalem organized themselves to pray, even though Peter's situation seemed hopeless. He was in prison, chained between two soldiers, guarded by four squads of soldiers, and scheduled for execution in just a few days. But even while they were gathered together, praying for Peter, God was answering their prayers. An angel releases Peter's bonds, whisks him through the prison, and leads him right through locked gates. When Peter pinches himself to see if he's dreaming, he realizes he's standing in front of the house of a Christian family, and goes up to knock on the door. What astonishment and joy there was for the believers gathered there that night, for God had performed a miracle in response to their pleas for help.

5. "But at midnight Paul and Silas were praying and singing hymns to God, and the prisoners were listening to them. Suddenly there was a great earthquake, so that the foundations of the prison were shaken; and immediately all the doors were opened and everyone's chains were loosed" (Acts 16:25–26, NKJV). While two men praised God and prayed, in the hearing of all the other prisoners, God miraculously set them free. This display of divine power must have been convincing, and surely brought glory to God. Many were saved that night (Acts 16:32–34).

6. "Pray that I will keep on speaking boldly for [God], as I should" (Eph. 6:20, NKJV). The mighty man of God, planter of churches and teacher of theology, sends out a humble request for prayer. "Pray that I will be bold enough to say what I should say, when I should say it." We all need prayer.

7. "Speaking the truth with love, we will grow up in every way into Christ, who is the head. The whole body depends on Christ, and all the parts of the body are joined and held together. Each part does its own work to make the whole body grow and be strong with love" (Eph. 4:15–16, NCV). The imagery is beautiful in the New King James Version: "The whole body, joined and knit together by what every joint supplies, according to the effective working by which every part does its share, causes growth of the body for the edifying of itself in love." We need one another. We are irrevocably intertwined. We are called to encourage and support one another—and we can do this in part through prayer.

8. "Be kindly affectionate to one another with brotherly love, in honor giving preference to one another" (Rom. 12:10, NKJV). Paul exhorts Christians to put the needs of one another ahead of our own. When we are praying for one another in a group setting, we need not fear how our words come out. The circle of united prayer is filled with kindness, affection, and love. No one will criticize your plain words to the Lord.

9. Even if you lack the confidence to pray out loud in a group setting, it doesn't mean you cannot participate in the prayer. Keep your mind alert, and follow the flow of the intercessions. Agree with the prayers being spoken. Add your own thoughts. Though they remain unspoken, God hears the prayers of your heart.

Chapter 9

1. A prayer warrior is anyone, man or woman, who is exercising the gift of intercessory prayer.

2. In Luke 2:37, we find the old widow woman, Anna, who blessed Jesus on the day he was taken to the temple to be dedicated. Luke says that at the age of eighty-four, Anna never left the temple. Night and day she worshiped God there, lifting up prayers and fasting. According to Acts 1:14, Mary the mother of Jesus and several other women met together continually for prayer (NLT). And in 1 Timothy 5:5, Paul declares that a true widow spends much time in prayer throughout her days and nights.

3. "He will rescue us because you are helping by praying for us. As a result, many will give thanks to God because so many people's prayers for our safety have been answered" (2 Cor. 1:11, NLT). Though our individual prayers may not seem like much, when the manifold prayers of believers are sent up on behalf of something, God responds. Someone I know calls this "blanketing" someone with prayer. And these prayers do help.

4. God gives each of us some little confirmation of His power and love. Whether the miracles are large or small, they serve to remind us of His availability, His nearness, and His willingness to act in our behalf. By doing so, He coaxes us away from relying so much on ourselves. He is teaching us to lean on Him for our every need.

5. "Dear brothers and sisters, I ask you to pray for us. Pray first that the Lord's message will spread rapidly and be honored wherever it goes" (2 Thess. 3:1, NLT). "Pray to the Lord who is in charge of the harvest; ask Him to send out more workers for His fields" (Matt. 9:38, NLT). We do not pray simply for our own health and comfort. Do you pray for the lost? Have you ever prayed that God will be glorified everywhere? Do you ever pray for the boys and girls who will one day be the leaders of the church? Do you pray for the Lord to call more young people into missions? Try broadening your horizons, and including these people in your prayers. You may never meet them on this side of heaven, but your prayers on their behalf are heard by God.

6. "Continue to pray as you are directed by the Holy Spirit" (Jude 1:20, NLT). When we come to God in prayer, we should always follow the Spirit's leading. Sitting in quietness, He brings to mind the people and places we should pray for. Someone will come to mind, "out of the blue," and this is your invitation to intercede for them.

7. "All night long I pray, with hands lifted toward heaven, pleading. There can be no joy for me until He acts . . . You don't let me sleep. I am too distressed even to pray" (Ps. 77:2, 4, NLT). When the Spirit lays a burden to pray on your heart, it is impossible to ignore. David, in his fervency, couldn't even sleep nights. The New King James Version says "You hold my eyelids open."

8. We are not off the hook! Of course we should pray. We are urged to constant prayer, fervent prayer, earnest prayer. Three times in Matthew 6:5–7, Jesus says, "When you pray . . ." It's not *if* or *should you find time to*, but *when* you pray. Prayer is a given in our Savior's mind. You may feel cautious, uncertain, or caught up in busyness right now, but who's to say God will not lead you into the gift of intercession as you reach some new season of life. He's full of surprises!

Chapter 10

1. For many churches, the following adjectives could sum up a room full of praying Christians: hesitant, repetitive, rambling, trite, limited, dry. Where there could be power, the prayers are filled with religious jargon and meaningless platitudes. On the other hand, many churches are filled with Christians whose prayers reach right to the throne of God—plain-speaking, Spirit-led, honest, reverent, persistent, bold.

2. First Kings 8:30 says, "May You hear the humble and earnest requests from me and Your people when we pray toward this place. Yes, hear us from heaven where You live, and when You hear, forgive" (NKJV). Through the Scriptures, effective prayer is described as earnest, fervent, and humble.

3. "The earnest prayer of a righteous person has great power and wonderful results" (James 5:16, NLT). The New King James Version puts it this way: "The effective, fervent prayer of a righteous man avails much." And the New Century Version simply says, "When a believing person prays, great things happen."

4. Yes. In a way, it does. Praying without ceasing involves putting our Heavenly Father at the forefront of our thoughts throughout our days. In the same way, living life in an attitude of prayer assumes we are in constant communication with God. His concerns, His glory, and His will have priority in our behavior, our choices, and our conversations. Both provide a basis for our relationship with God and with those around us.

5. Ezra 10:1—weeping and rolling around on the ground. Psalm 77:2—with hands lifted towards heaven. Mark 14:35—falling face down on the ground. Jonah 3:8—in sackcloth and ashes. Acts 6:6—laying on hands. Acts 9:40—kneeling. Acts 13:3—fasting, and laying on of hands. Acts 20:36—knelt down. 1 Timothy 2:8—assembled in a group, lifting up hands together.

6. We kneel in reverence and humility. We are servants, making petitions of our King, and we kneel to affirm His Lordship and our respect. We raise our hands in surrender. With open hands, we signal our neediness, our willingness, our expectation of His answer. We bow our heads in the presence of holiness. We are sinful, flawed, unworthy. We acknowledge the Father's preeminent place, and honor Him with our very posture.

7. I admit, there are times when we bow our heads for the closing prayer at church, and my mind drifts immediately to lunch plans. Even in the quiet of my home, wandering thoughts can interrupt prayer times. Though we might assume the proper pose, and count the minutes, a time of prayer is hardly worthwhile if our inner attitude is one of restlessness or distraction. Give the Lord your full attention.

8. "O Lord, hear my plea for justice. Listen to my cry for help. Pay attention to my prayer, for it comes from an honest heart" (Ps. 17:1, NKJV). We rush to the side of our loving Heavenly Father, saying, "Look at me! I have something I need to ask you! Pay attention to my request! It is so important!" And our loving Father always hears us out.

9. "For these people are stubborn rebels who refuse to pay any attention to the Lord's instructions" (Is. 30:9, NLT). Be sure your attitude of prayer maintains a balance of speaking and listening. God wants to hear from you, but He also wants you to hear Him!

Chapter 11

1. "I am praying to you because I know you will answer" (Ps. 17:6, NLT). We may not like to wait, and we may not like the answer when it comes— we may not even understand why we received the answer we did—but God will answer us.

2. "As I was praying, Gabriel . . . came swiftly to me . . . 'The moment you began praying, a command was given'" (Dan. 9:21–23, NLT). Even as Daniel was praying, a command rang out in heaven and the angel Gabriel was sent to speak with him.

3. "I prayed to the Lord, and He answered me, freeing me from all my fears" (Ps. 34:4, NLT). The God who can drive away our fears can do anything—anything at all. Though your trial may seem small and trivial compared to somebody else's, God will listen and He can answer. He may want to show you in a special way just how much He loves you.

4. "Whatever things you ask when you pray, believe that you receive them, and you will have them" (Mark 11:24, NKJV). This goes right along with the statement Gabriel made to Mary, "With God, nothing will be impossible" (Luke 1:37, NKJV).

5. "For I know that as you pray for me and as the Spirit of Jesus Christ helps me, this will all turn out for my deliverance" (Phil. 1:19, NLT). Paul's words echo that familiar verse in Romans: "All things work together for good to those who love God" (Rom. 8:28, NKJV). No matter what our situations might be, through our prayers for one another and the Spirit's working, no situation we live through will ever go to waste. God will use it to His glory somehow.

6. Receiving a "no" to the things we so desperately want can leave us hurt and confused. At the time, we wonder what God could be thinking. His refusal to give us what we want stings. But sometimes, later in life, we look back at that "no" and see it as a turning point. Though we could not know it, God's negative answer put us on a path rich with blessings. Through the outcomes, our faith was built up, and our Lord was glorified.

7. "Wait on the Lord; Be of good courage, And He shall strengthen your heart; wait, I say, on the Lord!" (Ps. 27:14, NKJV). The answer will come in God's own good timing. Take courage, for you know whatever comes, it will be for your good and His glory.

8. "Those who wait on the Lord Shall renew their strength; they shall mount up with wings like eagles, they shall run and not be weary, they shall walk and not faint" (Is. 40:31, NKJV). Even as our souls wait, God's Word gives us hope. God's Word has promised when we wait on the Lord, He will strengthen us. We need not feel hopeless, restless, or unsettled when we do not know all the answers.

9. "My soul, wait silently for God alone, For my expectation is from Him" (Ps. 62:5, NKJV). Silently, quietly, patiently, without murmuring or grumbling. Trusting, patient, relying on His sovereign plan.

10. "The Lord is good to those who wait for Him, to the soul who seeks Him. It is good that one should hope and wait quietly for the salvation of the Lord" (Lam. 3:25–26, NKJV). Seek God, hope in Him, wait quietly for His answer, and the Lord will be good to you.

Chapter 12

2. Paul says, "How thankful I am to Christ Jesus our Lord for considering me trustworthy and appointing me to serve Him" (1 Tim. 1:12, NLT). In Ephesians, Paul declares, "When I think of the wisdom and scope of God's plan, I fall to my knees and pray to the Father" (Eph. 3:14). Though we may pray often for our own needs, for the needs of others, and for God's glory to be revealed throughout the earth—we must never forget our manners, and say "Thank You" to God.

3. So often throughout his letters, Paul will say something like: "I have never stopped thanking God for you" (Eph. 1:16, NKJV). His love for his fellow believers is evident, and Paul's prayers are filled with thanksgiving for the friends and fellowship God has provided. Whenever Paul would pray for someone dear to his heart, he would couple his intercession with gratitude. "I always thank God when I pray for you, Philemon" (Philem. 1:4, NLT).

4. "Are any among you suffering? They should keep on praying about it. And those who have reason to be thankful should continually sing praises to the Lord" (James 5:13, NKJV). Our hearts are moved by the pains of others, and we join together in prayer for them. But seeing the struggles of our sisters in Christ can also serve to make us grateful for God's blessings in our lives.

5. The prayer of thanksgiving, made into a song for all to hear, brings glory to God because His wonderful works are shared with all who hear: "I will praise the name of God with a son. I will magnify Him with thanksgiving" (Ps. 69:30, NKJV). When we begin praying, thanksgiving is the place to start—opening our quiet times with a song of praise. "Let us come before His presence with thanksgiving" (Ps. 95:2, NKJV). How many of the praise choruses we love to sing in church are simply thank you notes set to music? Start collecting a list of them to keep in your Bible or prayer journal. "Sing to the Lord with thanksgiving; sing praises on the harp to our God" (Ps. 147:7, NKJV). When God works in our lives, they are transformed. Our wildernesses become gardens, and our sorrows are turned into joy. In our hearts, there will be "thanksgiving and the voice of melody" (Is. 51:3, NKJV).

6. "I raise my voice in praise and tell of all the miracles you have done" (Ps. 26:7, NCV). When we share our little stories of God's faithfulness, we encourage one another. For some of us, it changes our perspective—opening our eyes to how God really is showing us His love every day.

7. "As God's grace brings more and more people to Christ, there will be great thanksgiving, and God will receive more and more glory" (2 Cor. 4:15, NLT). Those who have become Christians, saved by God's grace, are so grateful for their salvation, they cannot help but share their excitement with others. In their gratitude, they tell everyone they know about their experiences—and God is glorified in the telling. When we tell others about God's work in our lives, He is glorified.

8. Well, back in David's time, literal sacrifices could be made in the Temple by those wishing to show God their thanks for His blessings. So when David says "I will offer to You the sacrifice of thanksgiving" (Ps. 116:17, NKJV), he is referring to the usual practice of showing proper gratitude by bringing an animal to sacrifice on the altar. But what about us? Have you ever considered thanksgiving to be a sacrifice? Consider this: Giving God the credit and the praise for the outcome of a situation in your life means acknowledging that you didn't do it on your own. Everything we have is a gift from God, and we sacrifice both our self-reliance and our self-congratulations when we tell Him thank you.

9. "Rooted and built up in Him and established in the faith, as you have been taught, abounding in it with thanksgiving" (Col. 2:7, NKJV). See how Paul describes our spiritual lives? Rooted in Christ. Built up in Christ. Established in the faith. And abounding with thanksgiving over all of it. Do you catch the note of enthusiasm there? Do you appreciate every facet of the Lord's work in your life? I hope I do.

10. "Amen! Blessing and glory and wisdom, Thanksgiving and honor and power and might, be to our God forever and ever. Amen." Our grateful hearts will never cease to sing the praises of our God. Amen!

Acknowledgments

© Clairmont, Patsy; Johnson, Barbara; Meberg, Marilyn; and Swindoll, Luci, *Joy Breaks* (Grand Rapids: Zondervan Publishing House, 1997)

© Clairmont, Patsy; Johnson, Barbara; Meberg, Marilyn; and Swindoll, Luci, *The Joyful Journey* (Grand Rapids: Zondervan Publishing House, 1998)

© Clairmont, Patsy, *The Best Devotions of Patsy Clairmont* (Grand Rapids: Zondervan Publishing House, 2001)

© Johnson, Barbara, *The Best Devotions of Barbara Johnson* (Grand Rapids: Zondervan Publishing House, 2001)

© Meberg, Marilyn, *The Best Devotions of Marilyn Meberg* (Grand Rapids: Zondervan Publishing House, 2001)

© Swindoll, Luci, *The Best Devotions of Luci Swindoll* (Grand Rapids: Zondervan Publishing House, 2001)

© Walsh, Sheila, *The Best Devotions of Sheila Walsh* (Grand Rapids: Zondervan Publishing House, 2001)

© Wells, Thelma, *The Best Devotions of Thelma Wells* (Grand Rapids: Zondervan Publishing House, 2001)

© Women of Faith, Inc., *We Brake for Joy* (Grand Rapids: Zondervan Publishing House, 1997)